The Sales Manager's Handbook

Getting the Results You Want

By

Joseph C. Ellers

www.joeellers.com

ISBN: 1-4033-6555-5 (e-book)
ISBN: 1-4033-6556-3 (Paperback)

Library of Congress Control Number: 2002111732

This book is printed on acid free paper.

Printed in the United States of America
Bloomington, IN

1stBooks – rev. 10/28/02

Dedication

To my loved ones

Acknowledgements

This book represents about a quarter century of sales involvement. Some of the concepts here are original, some are modified and some are probably stolen from others (not deliberately, you understand.) There are some people that I need to highlight for special thanks because the things they have taught me have been invaluable.

Nat Cain and Guerry Burnett hired me into my first sales job and taught me a lot more than even I was aware of at the time. Because of them, I know what professional sales looks like. At that first job, I was also part of what I still regard as the best overall sales team I have ever seen. Men like Bob Altier, Greg Fair, and Dan Tyner all took money out of their pockets (because they gave me their time) to teach me how to sell and I will never forget any of them.

My old friend and mentor, Art Zucker, is another guy that has to be singled out for thanks. He is a brilliant strategist and a great teacher and my decade of work with him has been one of the best experiences of my professional life.

Richard Russell and Ed Schueler are also on the list of people that have taught me things over the years and when they speak, I listen.

There are a whole bunch of people involved with the Chief Executive Network that I need to thank but the list is too long to put everyone in. In my work with that group, I have known all kinds of great company leaders who have given me a chance to work with them and who have also taught me a few things along the way. Specifically, I want to thank two of my fellow facilitators, David Campbell and Vic Leonino, for their wisdom and input. Thanks also go to Constance Wolfe for her excellent input. Special thanks also to Bob Grabill, the CEO of the Chief Executive Network. Bob not only contributed to this work with his foreword but also through his valued input and insights into how things really work.

Finally, there are two other people who need to be acknowledged: my colleagues, Paul Clipp and Jacqueline Reid. It has been my pleasure to work with both of these fine people for years. Jackie has helped me immensely with the "people" side of business equations and Paul has helped me shape many of the ideas presented here by his thoughtful questions and comments.

Having said all of this, I take full responsibility for the information here. If you don't like it, blame the author not these people that tried to make it better.

Joseph C. Ellers

Table of Contents

Foreword

Nearly two-thirds of my 30 year career has been spent in sales management and executive sales management. Surprisingly, in all of that time I never did come across a comprehensive book on sales management. There were no shortage of books on selling mind you, but not on sales management (not included here are a couple of books in the University library which were academic, largely irrelevant, and at best somewhat helpful if you were managing a sales force 75 years ago).

There is a simple reason why. Sadly, less than 10% of the managers and an even smaller number of sales people truly regard sales management as a profession. By profession I mean the same thing that it means to be a Doctor, Engineer, Lawyer, or C.P.A. In other words, a *science* as well as an art form to be practiced. Just as each of these professions requires licensing, periodic testing, continuing education, etc., so should this *profession.* Now I realize that while *licensing* might stir a debate among sales professionals, I am strongly advocating the same type of rigor involved here.

Ambitious yes. Necessary? Absolutely. (Imagine each C.P.A. working with their own definition of an income statement, a balance sheet, their own definition of a debit or credit?). But where do we start?

Fortunately, I met someone several years ago who shares my passion around this concept. I'm referring to Dr. Joseph Ellers, the author of this book. At the time, I was in my third year of building a nationwide Network for CEO's entitled the Chief Executive Network (CEN). Simply put, CEN utilizes a model in which top management can dramatically shortcut the learning curve on critical issues relevant to their business growth. At any rate, one of our manufacturing CEO's highly recommended Dr. Ellers to me as a potential facilitator for our process.

The rest is history as they say. Over the past five years, Joe has continually been one of our highest rated facilitators. This owes in no small part to his unique understanding of the total business process. In fact, it's his innate knowledge of business processes which naturally complements his practice of sales management and strategic consulting.

As you'll see from this book, Joe knows what he is talking about. Moreover, top management can use this book as a guide to assess whether they have a sales management process or are relying on "aura" of what they hope is good sales management. This I promise you: if you faithfully employ the principles here, you will dramatically improve both short and long-term profitable revenues for you company.

Enjoy!

Bob Grabill, CEO
Chief Executive Network

Section 1.0 Introduction

You might not have noticed but a few years ago, the accountants took over. Where before there had been pristine desks, covered only by coffee stains and exotic paperweights, desks suddenly became covered by reports. This is because <u>management</u> became synonymous with <u>measurement</u>. The first important distinction is that management is not about reading reports. Reports are measurement. They tell you what has happened and they give you insight into potential problem areas—but measurement is not management.

Section 1.1 Sales Management Defined

In fact, I want to propose a definition of management, for the purposes of our discussions together:

Management is creating systems that give you the ability to drive specific activities that support your goals. And the corollary is that you can intervene, in advance, when you do not like the activities. (Try and do that by reading reports about what <u>has</u> happened.)

We use this definition because this is what this book is all about:

Defining clearly what you want
Defining the specific activities required to get you there

Putting in monitoring systems to ensure that the activities are taking place
Measuring to see if the results match the desired ones

The bottom line on management involves activity. In this work, you will find hundreds of activities—things that you can do and things that you can direct others to do. The best thing about these activities is that they are field-tested and they work. As you read, you will nod in agreement at some of the information presented (and curse the author when he makes statements with which you vehemently disagree.) If it feels right, it's because you have done it before yourself. If you disagree, examine your disagreement. It's possible that the author does not understand the nuances of your business. It's also possible that you have a preferred way of doing things and don't want to be challenged.

The key questions is this: Do you want results that are different from what you are getting today?

If the answer to this question is "Yes," you will have to make at least one of these changes in your organization:

1) Do some things you have never done before
2) Do some things you are already doing more often
3) Do some things you are already doing differently

4) Stop (or significantly curtail) doing some things you are currently doing

As you go through this book, think about the things presented in this light. Appendix 1 is a list that you can fill out that reflects these four points. They will comprise your "Action items" from this book. Because if you want different results as a sales manager, you will have to do some things differently.

That's what life is all about. If you want different results, you need to drive different activities. And the best thing about activities is that they are completely under your control (as opposed to results). For example, every salesperson might not be able to guarantee that they can increase sales by 10% (result) but they can guarantee you that they will make 10% more sales calls (activity).

So your number one job is to make sure that your people are working on the "right things" as often as possible. To do this, you're going to have to start with a clear definition of "right." As you work through the materials in this book, you will be asked to make literally dozens of choices. Every time you make a choice, you make it clearer to your people what the "right things" are. This will make it easier for them to be successful and easier for you to manage their activities.

An example of this occurs in the next section when we ask you to answer a simple question: What do you want to sell? Think about the different impact on your sales efforts based on your answer. If your answer is "Everything we offer," you are providing no guidance.

3

If you say, "Focus on these three products/services for this quarter," you are managing.

Section 1.2 Sales versus Marketing

Let me be upfront, I am not going to talk a lot about marketing because marketing and sales are not the same thing. Many people, including a whole lot of professors and even a handful of real-life business executives, confuse the two. Marketing is the big picture that addresses research, your message, your product/service mix and your promotional activities. Sales is the attempt to take a piece of business that you do not currently have—generally from a competitor.

We confuse our people and ourselves by using titles such as Marketing Rep when what we really need is a Salesperson.

Selling is comprised of these <u>activities</u> (which we will elaborate on later in this masterpiece):

- Finding new customers to call on; either new organizations or new parts of existing customers

- Finding new people within organizations that control the buying decision for what you are trying to sell

- Finding "real" pieces of business where we can get an order

- Getting your organization/proposed solution qualified by the customer

- Making an offer to sell

- Getting a yes or no on an open piece of business

These are sales activities and all of the other things that salespeople do (or are asked to do) during the course of a day are non-sales activities. These non-sales activities could be: administrative, marketing, service or technical support. All of them are important but they are not sales activities.

For our purposes, we will focus on the "hardcore" sales activities—with a little marketing thrown in for the sales management to consider as a foundation for directing sales activities.

Section 1.3 Overcoming habits/creating new habits

At the root of sales management is the subject of habits. The greatest enemy of organizational success is the Law of Inertia put forward by Sir Isaac Newton. This Law states that what will occur is what is occurring now—unless acted on by an outside force. Your salespeople have habits. Some of them are good and some of them are not so good. As a sales manager, your job is to work with your people to overcome some old habits and to create some new ones.

Section 1.4 Proact versus react

The final philosophical point in sales management involves the very nature of your sales management effort. Do you proact or react? To proact means that you will make something happen. To react means that you will respond when something happens.

In sales, I strongly recommend the Plutonium Rule:

Do to the marketplace what you want to do.

Start with a clear picture of what you want to occur. Then structure activities designed to get you there. You might not succeed but at least you are moving the organization in a direction.

Many sales managers play the game of finding out what is happening and then responding. Some heavyweight champs are great counter-punchers but most of the great ones take the fight to their opponent. It's better to lead by telling people where to go than what to do when they are attacked.

Section 1.5 How to use this Handbook

The book is structured in such a way that it has many uses. If you're a sequential kind of person, you can start at the front and read it straight through. The book starts with the underlying strategic decisions you have to make, addresses organizational structuring decisions, people decisions, sales planning, the sales process, the sales call process, sales management tools, training and development and ends up with compensation. It ends up being a sequential step-by-step process that allows you to examine and make decisions about every part of your process—with one building on the one before. That's one approach.

You can also use it as a diagnostic tool. We have included a series of self-scoring tests for each section. If you are having difficulties in a particular part of sales management or you just want to add a few tools to your tool kit, read the section, score yourself and then decide what you want to start, do more of, do better or stop doing. In that way you can take a piece at a time and apply it.

We also put a series of forms and checklists at the back of the book. These can be used to supplement your efforts.

This book is meant to be used. Carry it with you. Reread a section every now and then. Write in it. Tear out pages if you need to. The greatest waste would be for you to take the time to read it, come up with a few ideas that you want to implement but never do anything about it.

Remember that if you want different results, you have to do different activities—it all starts with you.

Section 2. 0 Strategic Foundations

The first decision that every organization needs to make is simultaneously complex and simple. The questions are easy enough:

What do you want?
How do you want to get there?

But contained in these questions are some of the hardest decisions an organization ever makes. And because organizations do not really make decisions—people do—and because every person often looks at the problem somewhat differently, getting "real" answers to those two questions is often difficult. If you are in sales management, you have to have the answers to those questions—otherwise you do not really know what to do. Which products are more important than others? Which customers are more important than others? What orders need to be expedited?

If the organization is unclear on these questions—and sales management is unclear—then every day, the people in your organization will spend a lot of their time negotiating over these issues—rather than the things they need to be doing—like making and selling things.

The purpose of this section is to present a process that will help you to do one or more of the following:

Define your strategy
Refine your strategy
Translate the organizational strategy into a sales strategy

Once your strategy is clearly defined, many other decisions will become a lot easier to make—and to implement.

Section 2. 1 Overview

Sales management begins with a clear understanding of the strategy of the organization.

As a sales manager, it's your job to understand it, then to create sales plans that accomplish it, then to further break the plans down into specific activities that can be done on a regular basis. The first problem is that many organizations do not have clear strategies at the top. You're supposed to grow the business this year (like somehow this year is different?) Okay, how is it supposed to look? You've got a dollar target, maybe even by product or service and a gross margin target. You think that's a strategy?

Let's clear up the confusion with a few definitions. There are three different levels for you to consider:

Goals
Strategies
Tactics

Joseph C. Ellers

Dollar targets, as described above, are really goals. This is the top level of any strategic process. A key question is: How much profit do we want? The organization starts with that question and works backwards.

Strategies are what we will create to help us get to the goals. When we define the type of business we want **and** the customers we intend to get it from **and** our value proposition, we have a strategy. Is it all right for all of our sales to come from our existing customers or should 20% come from new customers? What percentage of sales need to come from new products or services? Why will the customer consider buying from us? These are the kinds of questions that must be resolved to create a strategy.

The third level involves the tactics. This is the step where we put together the specific activities required to accomplish our strategy. Many managers try to manage at the tactical level without the strategic underpinning. As an example, one sales manager assigned goals of five sales calls per day to each salesperson. This is a tactic but because there was no guidance on the customers to call on, the people to speak to inside the customers or the topics to discuss, this does not qualify as a strategy. (In fact, it might have been totally inappropriate for some territories. Ever tried to make five good calls in a day in North Dakota?)

A strategy really answers two key questions, "What do you want?" and "How do you want to get there?" (By the way, a good strategy also tells you **not** to do some things, so keep this in mind.)

The first strategic question is simple enough: What do you want? Think about this one a minute for your organization. How clear are you on the answer?

Let's get specific, how much growth are you supposed to produce by selling existing products into existing customers?

New products or services into existing customers?

What percentage of your growth is supposed to come from new customers? How much of this is supposed to come from the sale of new products or services?

If you could not immediately answer these questions, there is no strategy. Or to be more precise, you have a "retail" strategy where you theoretically want to sell everything to every one in whatever combination it comes along.

The most important thing for management to do is to answer this question and then make sure that everyone in the organization knows what the answer is. If you want to have some real "fun," go ask your salespeople the questions above and listen to their answers.

Their answers might be all over the board—for your company and even for their territories. So on a daily basis, they really have no idea what kind of appointments to set, who they really need to talk with or what they need to talk about.

The second key strategic question involves the "How?" **How** do you want to get there? Or, why will we be able to get additional business? The answer here involves the value proposition. This is a lot thornier than it sounds because most companies answer this question with answers that sound like this:

"We provide superior service."
"We bring innovation to our customers."
"We save our customers money."

Sounds really great but in almost every case, your growth will come at the expense of an existing competitor. In other words, someone already has the business you need to grow and you will have to displace them. How many of your competitors try to keep to their business by saying the following: "We provide lousy customer service, we haven't innovated anything since Hoover was President and we're expensive to boot?"

The sad fact is that your stated reason for taking business away from your competitor may be the very reason they are buying from that competitor now. You might not even be as good as the current competitor in the area you have chosen to compete in. Think about the challenge your salespeople face when they are making a call. They make a statement that sounds like this, "We want a chance to work with you because we provide excellent customer service." In every customer's mind, a blunt challenging statement roars out, "Prove it."

They may not say it, but they always think it and we almost never can.

An example of this might involve something like on-time deliveries. We say that we have a 98% fill rate. The customer asks you what the fill rates are for your top three competitors. And your answer is…You don't know. You know what you do but you have no idea how it really stacks up against your competition.

This is the second area that you must address as part of your strategy. You have to identify some very specific competitive advantages that you can prove to a current non-customer.

What's all this got to do with sales management? You might have a desire to skip this process, but do so at your peril. When we have been called in to clean up sales messes, a large percent of the time, a weak or un-communicated strategy is the root cause.

The recommendation is to address both of the following sections—Organizational Strategy and Sales Strategy. Begin by reviewing the strategy of your organization. (You might want to use the tools presented in the appendix to conduct a strategic planning meeting). Be warned that if your organization believes that all sales to all customers are "good," there will be some resistance to this effort.

After you are clear on the organizational strategy, use the second section to help you clarify the sales strategy for this year. (Later on, we will discuss how to roll out the sales strategy as part of the sales planning process).

Section 2.2 Organizational Strategy

In the previous section, we defined two key questions, "What do you want?" and "How do you want to get there?'

Let's begin by creating an answer to the first question. In the appendix, you will see a questionnaire and sample agenda to conduct a strategic planning meeting for your organization. Ideally, you would conduct some sort of strategic planning on an annual basis and this would provide the answers you need to create your sales strategy.

But, if you cannot do this exercise, take a few minutes and plot out the answers to the following series of questions:

What do you want to sell?

Assuming that your company sells more than one product or service, you have to define what you most want to sell.

You can decide the answer based on several different factors:

Profitability: Do you want to change the profitability of your organization by changing the focus on what you are attempting to sell? Do some products have better margins than others?

Market penetration: Can you open up some new market segments/customers by focusing on products that have applicability in those segments?

Competence: Do you want to focus on specific products that will give you enhanced credibility in a particular technology?

To answer these questions, you need to consider this:

What kinds of sales are most important for our business three years from now? Over the next year? Over the next 90 days?

Are your answers the same for all three? Do you need to begin positioning your company now to be successful in the future?

Using the strategic worksheet provided, identify the top five things your organization wants to focus on selling over the next year—in order. (Remember that some of the areas of focus may, in fact, be longer term). Do not put down generic answers like "service" or "quality." Instead list the things where you can send an invoice. Keep in mind that the focus products or services that you **need** to sell may not be the current top sellers.

After documenting your answers, take them to the rest of the management team and get their buy in. Start with agreement on the most important things for the salespeople to focus on selling. (We will, of course, continue to take orders for everything and will work on non-focus sales opportunities, but by listing what we **want** to sell, we are sending a message that there should be regular activities to support these strategically important items).

<u>Who do we want to sell it to?</u>

The next step is to define who you want to sell to. If your strategy implies that all customers are the same, you are not really directing the efforts of the salespeople and one call is as good as the next. The most limited commodity in any organization is time. Your salespeople have a limited number of sales calls they are able to make during the year. Where do you want them to focus their efforts? Are some customers more important than others? Are some prospects more important than others? How is importance defined? How clear are your salespeople on the kinds of customers we want to support the long-term vision of our organization?

Think a little about the characteristics of a good customer:

What business are they in?
How big are they?
Potential?
How are they organized?
Are they a public or private company?
What customers do they serve?
How do they position themselves in their markets?
Credit-worthiness?

Develop a profile of what a good customer looks like. Then, socialize your answer with the other members of the management team. Get their agreement. This is critical in that you want every part of the organization to support the same customers and prospects. For example, if your salesperson brings in two orders, which one is most important to get out (first)? Ideally, everyone in the organization is on the same page and supports the most important customers (and prospects) first.

Don't take the easy way out and designate your current top customers as the focus customers going forward. It might be that you most important future customers are not current customers—but should be.

What does a good order look like?

The third and final step is to be very clear on what a good order looks like.

Most salespeople will tell you that any order is a good order and I respectfully (almost) beg to disagree. We know that some orders are better than others.

Describe how a good order looks:

Two characteristics should be that it is something that you really want to sell to a customer that you really want to do business with. But take it one step further—how big is it? What is the minimum acceptable margin? How many line items are on it? What is the lead time? What kinds of put-ups, shipping, and handling are good for your organization?

Again, you have to socialize your answers with the rest of the management team. One of the facts of business life is that every organization has a "sweet spot" for orders. Your organization just naturally does certain orders better than others. (Note that your current sweet spot might not be where the market is. For example, if you want to make one thing all day long in 500,000 piece lots, you might be slightly out of step with your market if they want to buy 5 different items in quantities of 50 each). But, as an organization, you need to define good orders. And as with other discussions, this does not mean that other orders are "bad," although some of them probably are but that some orders are more desirable than others.

One of the little bits of sales management magic is that if you are very clear on what you want your people to work on, they begin to do more of it.

How do you want to get there?

One of the easiest things for an organization to do is to assume that they possess a competitive advantage. They think they do because their current customers tell them they do. What do you expect your current customers to tell you? However, every year a lot of your customers also tell you that you are not very good at some things. They do this by ordering less or not ordering at all.

If you want to gain some insight into your business, go survey the customers who had the largest decline in business with you over the last year and find out why. (Discount economic factors—find customers who are still doing a lot of business but just not with you). They may tell you that some of things you think are strengths **aren't.**

The most important activity in this section, however, is not the negative but the positive. Work with the top management team to create a clear statement of provable competitive advantage. What is it?

The goal here is to know how you will win additional business. Why will a current customer buy more of what they need from you? Or why will a prospect begin buying some of what they need from you?

Competitive advantage normally comes from addressing one of the issues listed below:

The Total Acquisition Cost (TAC) is less or

The Per Unit Cost (PUC) is less

Under the TAC side, there are a lot of factors:

High levels of technical support
JIT deliveries
Zero defects
Technological innovations
Inventory management programs
Superior customer service
(and more that you could list)

Under the PUC side, there is only one—your per unit cost is cheaper.

Either way, your organization needs to decide why you will win business in the long term. This decision will also drive other decisions such as where you invest your management time and organizational resources. What is your organization's competitive advantage?

And most important of all: Can you prove it to a non-customer before they give you an order?

Section 2.3 Sales Strategy

Once you have a clear understanding of the organizational strategy as ·defined in the previous section, you can begin the creation of a sales strategy. The key factor in sales strategy is growth. And as far as I know, there are only four ways to grow your business since both top and bottom line growth are determined by what you try to sell and who you try to sell it to.

Sell more of what you are already selling to customers you already sell to
Sell some new things to existing customers
Sell some of your existing products to new customers
Create some new products and sell them to new customers

Begin with strategic goal-setting

The box below is the Strategic Sales Growth Matrix. At the beginning of every year, you need to fill this out. (A copy is included in Appendix 2.) Take the "unreasonable" growth goal that you have been assigned and divide it among the boxes below. Remember to keep in mind the strategic issues you have already decided such as what you want to sell, who you want to sell it to and what a good order looks like.

	Existing products/services	New products/services
Existing Customers	Box 1*	Box 2
New Customers	Box 3	Box 4

*If a price increase is part of your growth strategy, put it in as part of Box 1.

Now that you have created a high level sales strategy, let's take a look at each box.

Box 1: Existing Products/Services and Existing Customers

To set a realistic target for this box, you have to understand the following things:

How much potential exists?
How much do you historically lose?
What is the potential for a price increase?
How much do you really want in this box?

How much potential exists?

The question of potential is the most important concept in sales (and I will return to it with boring regularity). If you want to grow business in this box, it has to exist. So the first question is, what is my current customer share? Note that we are talking about the percentage you have of available business in the customers you are currently working with.

(One quick way to get a handle on this is to look at what you quoted to those customers over the past year and compare this to the orders you actually received. It's not a great method but it will give you some indication of the potential).

How much do you historically lose?

If you look at your customer list three years ago and then compare what happened last year, you might notice some changes in the top group. Some customers rise, others fall and others disappear entirely. This is normal. You need to know, roughly, how much business you normally lose every year in this group so that you can know how much you have to make up. (Or, if the losses are not understood, you might decide to find out why and focus on retention for a year to see if you can keep more of what you already have).

To do this:

Identify the number of customers that generated 80% of your total sales 3 years ago. Calculate the total sales dollars for that group. Take the same customers and look at the volume of sales they did last year. Was the number up, down or flat?

What is the potential for a price increase?

You need to look at the potential for a price increase. I know that it's a dirty word these days, but there may be some instances where you can get back some of what you just lost in the calculation above by simply raising prices. Are there market conditions that justify a price increase?

If the market conditions do not exist, sometimes they do exist within a group of your customers. Look at the customers that comprised the bottom 10% of your sales for last year. Look at the average sales price for those customers (or average gross margins). Since some of those people use you only as a last resort, you might be able to raise prices on some of those customers.

How much do you really want in this box?

The last consideration for Box 1 is, in fact, the most important: how much do you really want in this box? For example, if your company sold leather in 1900, your top 10 customers might have been makers of horse-drawn carriages. But if you were looking at your business, you would **not** to be focused on those customers because auto makers and carriage makers are not always the same people. Are any of your current customers on the technology bubble? Are some of them strongly considering outsourcing part of their business to a place that you cannot get to? What percentage of your sales efforts this year should be devoted to finding some new customers?

Box 2: New Products/Services and Existing Customers

After Box 1, the easiest way to grow your business is in Box 2. Again, if you sell more than one kind of product or service, and you have existing customers that either can or do buy more than one of your outputs, there is potential there. This assumes that these are customers you want and that the additional products that you sell are "good" products, as defined by your super-sleek strategy.

The first question is to try and determine how much potential (there's that word again) exists for additional products in your existing customer base.

One way to do this is to look at the connectivity of your products and services. For example, if a customer buys $10,000 worth of Widget A, how likely are they to use Widget B? And further, for every $10,000 of Widget A they buy, how much of Widget B should they use? (Not all products connect, but some of yours should. Isn't that why you sell them)?

This box is also important if your organization is developing new products or services to support current customers. If we offer it, how much potential exists in our current customer base?

Either way, you have to determine not only the amount of sales you want in this box but also the viability of gaining the number. For example, do you have to capture 95% or 1% of the existing potential to meet your sales targets of 5% growth? One of those numbers looks more realistic than the other.

Box 3: Existing Products/Services and New Customers

This is a "marketshare" question. To answer this question, you have to have some understanding of how much of the potential marketshare you have for all of your existing products/services.

For a great many businesses, true marketshare calculation is a waste of time. A better marketshare calculation is to pick a group of prospective customers and make some calculations about what their potential for your products might be. As an example, in your current customer base, you might know that for every million dollars of their product they make, they buy about $10,000 worth of your product. If you can find out the approximate annual sales of a prospective customer, you can do this calculation.

Again, the assumption is that the customers in Box 3 are the kind you want and that you can sell them the kinds of products/services that both you and the customer want.

Again, answer these two questions: How much business do you want in this box? Is it attainable?

Box 4: New Products/Services and New Customers

By far the most expensive, difficult (add any other adjectives that mean a pain in rear end here) box is Box 4. In Box 1, there are no variables. Your people understand both the customer and the product. In Boxes 2 and 3, there is one variable each. In Box 2, you know the customer but the product is "new." In Box 3, we know the product but the customer is "new." In Box 4, we are talking about creating new products and selling them to new customers.

Some businesses always have to have significant dollars in this box because their products are obsoleted or simply because their strategy is to diversify by using new products to open up new customers.

Once you have completed this matrix, your strategy is now complete. You have set overall sales targets for the following:

Existing products/services to existing customers
New products/services to existing customers
Existing products/services to new customers
New products/services to new customers

And you did this keeping in mind the overall strategy of your organization involving what you want to sell, who you want to sell it to, what a good order looks like—and the competitive advantage of your organization.

It may not be easy but now your sales strategy is clear—and more manageable—which is the point of this whole deal, right?

Sales Management Self-Audit

Rate each answer on a scale of 1-10 with 1 being "Not at all" and 10 being "Totally."

_____We have a defined organizational strategy that is known by all.

_____We have a specific, prioritized list of products/services we will focus on over the coming year.

_____We have a specific, prioritized list of customers/prospects (by territory) we will focus on over the coming year.

_____We have defined good orders within our organization.

_____We have a defined competitive advantage for each of our focus products/services that is known by our sales people.

_____We can prove our competitive advantage to prospective customers—even before they give us an order.

_____We know our customer share.

_____We know how much we historically lose.

_____We know the potential in our target prospects.

_____All of this is written down in one place.

Add your numbers and give yourself a score: _____.

Section 3.0 Sales Organization

The second major consideration for any sales organization involves the way you will organize your sales team. You probably inherited a sales organization that was organized a certain way. This style of organization was (hopefully) based on a set of market conditions. Your mission is to look at the market conditions that currently exist and see if they still drive the same kind of organization.

This is important because different types of organization will get certain results better than others. And the organization that you select also will drive the kind of people you hire—and this will affect the management style that you use.

Ideally, the sales organization should support the sales strategy. As an example, if your strategy involved providing high levels of technical support to customers in the field, you would probably not hire high school dropouts and put them on a phone bank. Instead, you would probably hire some sort of engineer with previous field experience. The problem that many sales managers have is that the sales organization they have is not reflective of their strategy. Many sales organizations are holdovers from earlier days when even the definition of the sales needs were different than what is needed today.

Success comes from aligning what you say you want to do with your organization and this involves making a series of choices—not only about the way you organize the sales effort but also the kinds of people you hire.

Section 3.1 Overview

Sales versus service versus technical support? Every sales organization has to make a choice regarding how it will impact the market. There are three distinct choices. A sales organization is one that is focused on booking new orders. Copier salespeople would be the extreme example of this type of selling where you sell a customer once a year (or less). A service organization is one that is heavily focused on providing a regular routine of visits to an established group of customers. Many distribution sales organizations are really service organizations. The final example involves a technical support organization. These people do not necessarily book new orders and they might not make a lot of routine calls but they are problem-solvers who work with customers to solve specific problems. (A focus on design wins that ultimately result in orders is an example of this approach.)

Hybrid solutions also exist which include the use of some centralized backup services which we will discuss as a subset of this section.

Geographic, market or product segmentation? The second consideration involves the kind of territories that make the most sense. Again, you have three choices. Geographic segmentation is often used because it allows salespeople to move quickly from

30

one customer to another. Market segmentation is used when you want salespeople to specialize on specific kinds of customers, such as automotive. Product segmentation would be used where you have a specialist that only sells certain types of products.

There is nothing wrong with having some of each but you need to decide what you really want because it would be difficult to assign a salesperson a geographic territory and then tell them to focus only on a specific type of customers and products. Something has to give in this circumstance. (As manager, you need to decide what.)

Direct, reps or distributors? Another consideration for the sales organization involves the type of representation you use. Do the employees work only for you, as in the case of direct salespeople? Are they semi-employed by you, as in the case of a manufacturer's rep who cannot represent competing products or do you go through distribution which generally allows for competitive products side-by-side? (Some businesses use all three and this may come as a surprise but there are distributors who have reps working for them so these lines are not as hard and fast as you might think.)

Inside, outside or both? Yet another organizational consideration involves whether you use inside salespeople (which would include four different types—counter sales, customer service, inside sales or telesales); outside sales (which could include any of the three main types of salespeople listed in the first section); or some combination of the two.

As with all of the other choices, you get a different set of results when you decide how you want to present to the market. If you want more walk-in traffic, you should have resources devoted to that section of the business. If you want to discourage it, you should probably close your counter operation.

A second organizational consideration here involves how you will team these different groups (if you have more than one) or if you decide to team them at all. And again, different approaches will yield different results.

Workload? The final major consideration involves the workload that you intend to give to each of these groups because you get a different kind of customer service when you assign 10,000 customers than you get when you assign 50.

Many sales organizations preach high levels of customer interaction while assigning hundreds of accounts to an outside salesperson. You have probably already guessed that it might not happen. Many sales organizations think they are getting one type of sales effort but undo it through the workload assigned to their salespeople.

The bottom line on all of these discussions is that you need to make conscious decisions about your sales organization and do everything that you can to ensure that the organization you are managing is structured to bring the results you want.

Section 3.2 Sales, Service or Technical Support

One of the most basic decisions that a sales manager needs to make is to decide whether the sales organization's orientation is primarily sales, technical support or service. Many of you are scratching your heads right now and rereading the preceding sentence. Aren't all sales organizations oriented to sales, you are probably asking?

In fact, many sales organizations (strategies) are not predicated on salespeople. In its simplest form, a salesperson should spend more than half of their time actually trying to book an order. (This does not mean to close a sales, per se, but the activities associated with finding new customers, finding new sources of decision-making authority inside customers, finding specific pieces of business, and trying to convert them into orders.) Huge numbers of salespeople spend less than 25% of their time in doing the activities defined above. The rest of their time is spent on handling service problems or providing technical support within existing accounts.

There is no question that these activities often lead to other sales but consider the difference between a copier salesperson and an industrial distributor salesperson. The copier salesperson calls on businesses all day long with one primary goal in mind—booking an order. Once the order is booked, the salesperson moves on to the next account—leaving the on-going account management to a supply salesperson that follows along in their wake. An industrial distribution salesperson, on the other hand, has a group of accounts and they are expected to routinely "service" these accounts. They provide technical support, training and old fashioned customer service in their account base.

To many managers, it seems obvious that if you sell it, you should also service it, but there are other models. Many great salespeople are killed when they go out and establish a great customer base. Rather than allowing someone else to provide the day-to-day service required to keep the business going, these people then become service people, based purely on the number of interactions they have to handle just to serve their existing customers.

Have you ever noticed that some of the best salespeople you have sometimes reach a plateau? They just cannot seem to get over a certain dollar amount. (Part of this may be due to lack of motivation. Some compensation plans penalize people for growing their territories and we know of some organizations that cut territories in half when they reach a certain amount of sales.) But often, this is simply due to lack of time. If a salesperson has seventeen places that they think they have to visit every week (to service), they really do not have much time left over to sell.

Even if you are in an industrial distribution business, you still have the option of having two different types of salespeople. You could have one type that strictly focuses on new opportunities and others who maintain on-going business. Or you could hire an assistant to the salesperson to handle the details. On one occasion, a salesperson grew their territory to over $10 million and the company hired an assistant and the territory grew to $17 million—all because they did the right thing and did not punish the salesperson for success.

Begin by defining the types of territories that you need:

Sales. The main goal in this type of territory is to grow the business. You believe that you can gain additional significant pieces of business by having people in the field that spend most of their time selling. An obvious example of this would be a pioneering territory with a low technical support need. There is little business to maintain so you really need someone to spend most of their time beating the bushes.

Service. The main goal of this territory is to help your customer base by resolving a myriad of logistics issues such as scheduling. You believe that you can gain additional significant pieces of business by having people in the field that spend most of their time in service activities.

Technical Support. The main goal in this territory is to help your customer base to understand (and use) your product. You believe that you can gain additional significant pieces of business by having people in the field that spend most of their time providing technical support.

To further complicate this issue, you could even have different needs in different sales territories. The problem is that most sales organizations have been established with the underlying assumption that all of your territories need the same kind of sales resource.

Take just a minute and mark the chart presented below. Put your mark at the spot (anywhere on or in the triangle) that represents the overall needs of your organization:

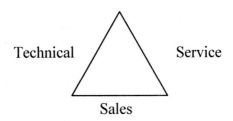

Technical   Service

Sales

You can mark it on the sales line—slanted either toward technical or service. Or you can mark it on the service line—slanted either toward sales or technical. Or you can mark it on the technical line—slanted either toward service or sales. Or you can mark it inside the triangle to indicate the approximate mix of all three. (Be careful because the more you try to make your sales force good at—the less likely they are to be good at anything—unless you supplement them with strong support services.)

Now, mark it again, this time based on where you think your organization is today. (Okay, you can also decide where each territory is if you want to do it individually.) The bottom line, however, is that your organization is known as one on of these things. Is it the right one?

Centralized services

Regardless of the style of organization that you have, you always have the option of creating centralized service bureaus to supplement the skills you need the most. The good thing about this approach is that it allows you to have a pretty homogenous work force because you are supplementing weaknesses with additional people resources. The bad thing about this is that you have two (or more) salespeople calling on an account and there is an additional cost to this approach.

Centralized services can be found in the following areas:

Customer service (Often covered with inside people)
Technical support (Field application engineers or technical support hotlines come to mind)
Sales (Specialists focused on specific products or specific markets/customers)

Centralized customer service exists in a lot of organizations. In fact, a lot of organizations think they have a field sales force supported by an inside staff of customer service people. (Sadly, many of these sales forces are outside service people supported by inside service people so they're not really getting what they

Joseph C. Ellers

want). Giving someone a sample bag and a car allowance does not make them a salesperson.

You have the option of providing centralized technical support such as Field Application Engineers. This approach is very common in some industries where there is a "relationship-type" salesperson who calls on a "propeller-head," when needed.

You have the option of providing super salespeople to supplement the work of a field sales team that is generally focused on service or technical issues.

To execute your sales strategy what kind of organization do you have? What kind do you need? Do you need to supplement it with some centralized support? What changes do you need to make, over time, to make it more reflective of your strategies?

Section 3.3 Geographic, market or product segmentation

Once you have decided the primary emphasis of the sales organization, the next step is to decide how to divide your customers and prospects. There are three main types of sales territory—geography, market and product segment. There are other varieties out there, like one, for instance, where one inside salesperson handles all accounts that begin with and A to M and another person handles calls from N-Z. This is really a derivation of the geographic division because it really doesn't matter who the customer is or what they want to talk about.

The fourth territory plan is called Rest of the World (ROW) and is a derivation of the other three. Each method has pros and cons. There is no one kind of organization that is "right." The question you need to answer as a sales manager is—What kind of organization is right, given the strategy and the salespeople that you currently have to work with? Consider each of these explanations and decide where you are and where you should be:

Geography

Many sales organizations segment customers and prospects by geography. There are very good reasons for doing this. There are also numerous sales strategies where this makes no sense.

In the past, we have almost always assumed that geographic segmentation is required if you have a field sales force. This assumes that the key factor is the amount of time between visits for outside salespeople. This is only true, however, if the primary sales strategy is face-to-face customer service or on-going technical support. There have also been changes in the way that customers view sales (and changes in technology provide other options, too.) that make this choice not an "automatic" any more.

The "cons" to this approach are that it assumes that salespeople can be an expert on every business they call on and that there are a lot of <u>important</u> customers in the same geographic area. Since neither of these may be true, there are some drawbacks to this approach.

Market Segmentation

The second choice involves organizing by market segment or customer. In this arrangement, you assign a salesperson/sales team specific responsibility for calling on paper mills or electrical contractors, for example. This team is expected to have intimate knowledge of a particular industry and the attendant problems. They should also have a better understanding of how your product or service applies to these applications and perhaps even a heightened sense of the competitive advantage that your offering has in that market.

The "cons" to this approach are that there may be long stretches of time between sales calls and, potentially, a lot of customers will not be called on at all—at least by outside salespeople unless you duplicate sales costs and have two different salespeople calling on the same territory.

Product Segmentation

The third way to segment your organization is to organize around products. The pharmaceutical industry will often have multiple salespeople calling on the same customer (although often not the same people within the account) because each is a specialist in a specific product.

This allows for an intense level of product/service knowledge and theoretically an almost expert knowledge of how your offering would be used within a given customer.

The disadvantage of this approach is that you might have to have multiple salespeople calling on the same accounts.

ROW

There is one other method of territory organization that has specific pros and cons. It is called the Rest of the World (ROW) territory and is generally a variation of the geographic segmentation—although it can be used in any organization plan. The ROW territory is one that is carved from other existing territories— normally on accounts where the suspected potential is either low or unknown. A rookie salesperson is often assigned this territory as a training ground—and, occasionally, the rookie will find a lot business and build a real territory because they do not know that there is not supposed to be any potential there. (This method is often used when transitioning inside salespeople to outside salespeople because it is a tough assignment.)

Decide where you want your sales organization to be. Mark the chart with where you want to be—and where you think you are.

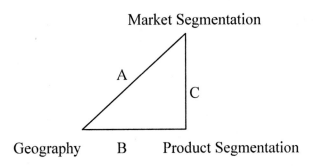

If your orientation is currently geographic, you could choose to move three different directions:

Toward market segmentation (Movement along the A line)
Toward product segmentation (Movement along the B line)
Toward a market segmentation with a product focus (Movement to the C line)

Or you have the option of marking inside the triangle and defining a need that will cause your organization to either behave in a schizophrenic fashion or provide centralized support or some other form of duplicate coverage.

If your goal is to move your organization toward market segmentation, you can:

Create one specialist and do a test market. Do sales increase in the target market? How many customers can a specialist handle? What is the payoff? Additional cost versus additional return?

If your goal is to move toward more product specialization, you could try the same approach.

The most difficult change would be to move to market/product segmentation (C line.)

This would mean completely recasting everyone's job role and would probably cause a little bit of anxiety. This would mean that everyone was either a market specialist or a product specialist and that there would be a lot of shared accounts and/or duplicate travel.

Think about this one carefully—although it can work well.

Remember that you have some choices here—you do not have to be all or nothing. You could have a sales force that is primarily geographic supported by market or product specialists. This will raise some issues about duplicate travel costs, account control and compensation for sales within shared accounts, but it might be the right strategy for your organization— based on what you are trying to accomplish.

Section 3.4 Direct, Reps or Distributors?

Of all the strategic organizational decisions, this one appears to be the easiest to make because organizations seem to be playing a continual game of musical chairs with the elements described above.

As with all of the other factors, there are very good reasons to use each of the approaches—and many reasons why each of them is less than appropriate—given a specific set of sales objectives.

Sadly, most of the decision-making process here seems to driven by cost containment and not strategy.

The simplest method for any sales organization is to have a direct sales force. Whether you are selling widgets or engineering services, there is a lot of comfort in having some salespeople that are yours. You can give them specific goals, make them attend sales meetings, put your brother-in-law on the staff (how did that get in there?), and generally feel good about the fact that you are in charge.

That's the good news. The bad news is that a direct sales force is a huge cost and if it is not managed correctly, you do not seem to get much for your investment. For this reason, many organizations have decided that sales is not one of their core competencies and have decided to outsource (at least) part of this function.

Using manufacturer's representatives and distribution is an outsource. You are outsourcing part of your sales and customer service costs (and in some industries technical support costs, as well) when you use either (or both) of these channels. The assumption is that you are using reps or distributors to get something that you cannot get by using a "captive" sales force. What do you gain by this move?

Some organizations even hire reps until the business in the territory reaches a threshold that allows the company to hire an individual whereupon they fire their rep.

(These same companies are often surprised to find that sales do not grow. Maybe its because you fired the salespeople and put a service/technical support person out there to support the book of business that was created by the rep.)

The above example is not intended as an endorsement for reps. In fact, there are many cases where reps are a bad idea, but remember that a rep is an outsource. You are not paying for something. You are trading lower costs for lower???? You have to fill in the question marks. In some cases, you get less attention than you would with your own people or less product knowledge or less service. That's what you wanted, remember? If you could make money in the territory by having full-time dedicated sales resource, you would have done so, right?

The same equation holds when you use distribution. Distributors are an essential part of the supply chain and they add value. They are an outsource for the following:

Inventory costs
Money costs
Transportation costs
Sales costs
Service costs
Production costs

As with reps, however, you are giving up something when you use distribution channels. You are potentially giving up product knowledge, customer knowledge and maybe even getting a less proactive salesperson. (All my disti pals need not get up in arms about this statement because some of the best salespeople in the country work for distributors, but you get the point).

As with many of the other features of sales organization, there are underlying assumptions about your marketplace that produced the way you are organized. Are those conditions still present? Do you need the same mix of the elements?

Begin by defining the way you want to use each of these channels:

	Percent of sales desired though channel
Direct	
Reps	
Distribution	

Now, mark the chart below based on where you want to be and where you are now.

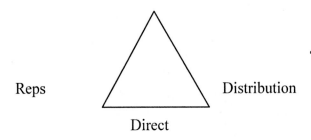

Reps   Distribution

Direct

The question really has four parts:

Does the organization need to move toward direct sales efforts?

Does the organization need to become more dependent on reps?

Does the organization need to become more dependent on distribution?

Does the organization need to use the rep/disti combination more?

Remember, too, that this question cannot be answered in a vacuum. You have already been asked to address the following elements:

Sales versus technical support versus service
Geography versus market or product segmentation

These two questions were asked first because you cannot make a decision on using reps and distributors unless you have first carefully considered these two questions (although a lot of organizations do.) Secondly, you cannot decide on which reps and distributors to use unless you have addressed these two issues.

So if you are in the electronics business and you need geographically-based technical support, reps might be the right answer. But if you need market-based service, they might not be part of the answer, at all. Making decisions like this are why they pay you the big bucks, I guess.

Section 3.5 Inside, Outside or Both

Having made all of the decisions listed above, you are now ready to decide whether you need to deploy your sales resources in the field or in your office—or both. (Or whether you need to use reps/distributors whose organizations match your profile.)

Despite the generally-accepted wisdom, there will always be some level of selling that requires personal face-to-face interaction.

In the 1800s, people were saying that the telegraph would eliminate the need for the field salesperson. In the early 1900s, they said the same thing because of the telephone. The late 1900s gave us teleconferencing and the Internet—all of which were supposed to eliminate the need for field salespeople. It may happen but I'm not betting against the world's truly oldest profession.

How dependent is your product/service's success on the need for people to go somewhere and look at a problem and coordinate answers from different groups of people? If this need is high, then you need a field sales force. You also need a field sales force if your business is about taking new pieces of business. Despite all of the technological advances, there are still a lot of people who are not comfortable in putting their career in the hands of people on the other side of a box—be it the phone, crt (or in some antiquated cases, the fax machine).

And we never need to forget that asking a customer to change from their present supplier to us is a personal risk as well as a business risk because if we fail, they fail.

So, if the sale is complex or requires a high comfort level (as is often the case when we try to switch business), we probably need some outside salespeople. (Remember that they can be technical, sales, service, rep, distributor, direct, geographic, market or product—what a list of choices!)

In businesses where service (on-time deliveries, product in stock) is the real driver and the products required are bought in small quantities, then you can have few (if any) outside salespeople.

Mark the line based on which is most relevant to your strategy:

Inside---Outside

The need for inside salespeople never seems to be in question and I have seen very few businesses that have outside salespeople, only, although they do exist. But if we accept the need for inside salespeople, the question becomes: What kind of inside salespeople do we need? (We will discuss this more in the next section, as well.)

Generally, there are four different types:

Counter sales. Many organizations have places where customers can come and buy things. If this is a necessary part of serving your key customers, you will offer this and staff it with retail-type people. (They might be technically competent and a lot of other things but they need to have some basic retail skills if they are going to interact with the public on a regular basis).

Customer service. Many organizations are confused about the difference between telesales, customer service and inside salespeople. Let the following few sentences be your guide. Customer service people are reactive. When the phone rings they pick it up and deal with whatever is on the other side. They will make outbound calls but normally in response to inbound calls. They may have assigned accounts and may do some cross-selling and upselling but they do not generally initiate a sales call. If over half of the time is spent reacting versus proacting, the job is defined as customer service—even though they might issue quotes and close orders. These people might have hundreds of customers.

(Note that this is not to be confused with the other customer service job of handling complaints or looking into orders or credits. There are people who do this job but it is not a "sales" job at all. The people who handle customer calls at American Express are a good example of this particular job.)

Telesales. A word that I dislike is telemarketing because it does not accurately describe the job. A telemarketing job would be conducting market surveys over the phone as opposed to telesales which is what most people really mean when they say telemarketing. (Telemarketing just sounds better to the kids who just graduated with a marketing degree.)

A telesalesperson is someone who makes a hundred outbound calls per day and tries to accomplish a specific task on each call. This might be to get the customer to look at a piece of literature or place an order. Telesalespeople do not have territories, as such, they are pretty much transaction-driven. They may call the same customers or prospects repeatedly but they are not really responsible for the customer. Further, they are not expected to answer inbound calls because their only mission is to make outbound calls.

Inside Sales.

An inside salesperson is someone who has a limited number of assigned accounts and is expected to make outbound calls on a regular basis and to sell things to these customers. They are a lot like outside salespeople who just happen to do their selling from inside your office. The key here is that these positions require people to spend most of their time proacting—calling people up and trying to sell something rather than waiting for the phone to ring. But they have account responsibilities, unlike telesalespeople, so they also do take inbound calls from customers.

A few words about remote salespeople: Whether they are inside or outside people, you need to remember that off-site salespeople need more management than those under your direct view. You should regularly review items such as phone records and mileage statements to ensure that they are really working. Even the best salespeople sometimes get a little slack when they are based out of their homes. I speak from experience, here. So help them to stay on track by regularly monitoring their activities and providing feedback about what you observe.

Now, with all options before you, what kind of inside salespeople do you really have? What kind do you really need?

Counter sales—customer service—telesales—inside sales

Partnerships

The final consideration involves how you will structure the interaction between your inside and outside salespeople. Do you want to pair them up? Or have a cluster of outside salespeople generally supported by another cluster of inside people?

To answer this correctly, you have to think back over all of your previous answers, especially your strategy.

If your goal is to provide seamless customer service to your key accounts, you should probably use some sort of dedicated pair arrangement where all of an outside salesperson's accounts are supported by one inside salesperson. (This does not mean that you have a 1:1 ratio of inside to outside.) It could be that one inside person would support as many as three outside salespeople but what we are saying here is that you get better customer service and account knowledge if an outside salesperson relies on one inside salesperson to support their key customers. In this way, the two of them can create and execute strategies on shared accounts rather than have the outside salesperson have to go to four or five different people to communicate about the key activities at the key accounts.

A strategy that lets a customer get multiple inside salespeople assumes that there is little value in building relationships from the inside. It also assumes that there is little need in understanding the specific activities of a given customer.

Based on your strategy, what should your inside/outside pairings look like?

Formal pairs------------------------------Random access

Section 3.6 Workload

As a sales manager, your salespeople get different messages based on the size of the territories. If you assign an outside salesperson 300 accounts, you are telling them to have superficial relationships with almost all of their accounts. If you assume that a true sales relationship (not service or technical support) requires at least 2 calls per month (and that the average outside salesperson can make 20-25 sales calls per week, you are really setting a territory limit of about 50 accounts. (50 weeks x 25 calls divided by 24 calls per year, per account).

Assume 300 accounts and the salesperson can call on an account once per quarter. Assume 150 accounts and you get a call every 6 weeks. Assume 75 accounts and you get a call every three weeks. (My definition of a "real" sales call is one that takes time. A salesperson can make a couple of thousand calls a year if they are all "howdy" or service type calls but if you want them to stop long enough to sell something, the number of makeable calls goes down dramatically.)

The same also holds true for an inside salesperson. The amount of accounts that you assign will dramatically affect the activities of the salesperson. Inside salespeople who have 300 assigned accounts are probably customer service people.

The important consideration here is for you to look at everything you decided about your sales team and see if you have assigned them the right number of accounts. Do you have outside salespeople with 250 accounts? Then they are really service people. Do you have an inside customer service person assigned to 50 accounts? That person might be able to function as inside sales.

Where are you? Does it reflect your strategy?

Inside

Few assigned accounts--------Many assigned accounts

Outside
Few assigned accounts--------Many assigned accounts

Sales Management Self-Audit

Rate each answer on a scale of 1-14 with 1 being "Not at all" and 14 being "Totally."

_____We have a defined sales focus: sales, technical support or customer service.

_____We have a defined sales focus regarding geographic, product or market segmentation.

_____We are clear on our use of direct, reps and distribution.

_____We have a clear understanding of our use of inside/outside salespeople.

_____The inside sales role is clearly defined.

_____The inside/outside partnership is structured appropriately.

_____The workloads correspond with our desired results.

Add your numbers and give yourself a score: _____. (Add back the 2 points I took away from you in the scoring process for being a model student.)

<u>Section 4.0 Sales Personnel</u>

In the previous section, we outlined the most important questions to address as you organize the sales effort. Once you have decided on the best sales organization, the next discussion involves staffing it with the right people. As with organization, you probably have had little choice about the salespeople you have. You probably inherited several of them. In many cases, your salespeople are really good and this can be a blessing and a curse because you may be looking to those people as a model when you need to add or replace members of the sales team.

In some cases, this may be appropriate but in other instances, it might not be as appropriate. Veteran salespeople often get good results because of longevity. The people they knew when they started have grown gray in the organizations they serve. Over time, their contacts have acquired promotions and power and these relationships, alone, may be the reason for their success. If you were to move them into a new territory, they might fail miserably because the business is significantly different from when they started. (They might also blow you away with the higher numbers they get.)

This discussion is not about whether your veterans are good or not, but about the kinds of people you need to add when you have the chance—or when the need arises. As with everything else, we want you to make a conscious decision, based on the strategy that you have determined is best for your organization.

Before reading this section, review all of the decisions that you have made about your strategy and your sales organization. What kind of salespeople do you need?

Section 4.1 Overview

One factor that is very important is to understand the proactivity that will be required of your sales team. This amount can vary dramatically, based on your strategy, but you have to very clear on what you want and hire to that level—especially if you want to change the level.

There are various levels of proactivity. Proactivity (in sales) means making an attempt to change what the customer does now or is planning to do. The scale looks something like this:

0	8
Totally Reactive	Totally Proactive

Totally Reactive. A totally reactive salesperson is generally the lowest level of inside customer service. (But I have seen outside salespeople who behave this way as well). They respond when asked and give the customer exactly what they ask for. If the customer wants a quote on 3 widgets, they provide it—promptly, maybe even cheerfully—but no more. The problem is that there is a quantity discount at 5 widgets and the customer is not aware of it. Proactive Rating 0

The next level is to take the inbound request and do something with it. This would be telling the customer about the quantity discount at 5 widgets, for example (upselling). This is also the part of the process where a salesperson might even ask if they needed 3 gadgets to go with their 5 widgets (since a person that needs widgets generally needs gadgets. This is also known as companion or matrix selling. Proactive Rating 1

We see lots of examples of this in our every day lives. When you go through a drive through window at your local grease emporium, the acne-challenged person on the other end of the microphone often asks if you would like to supersize your order (quantity discount) and they often ask if you would like "fries with that?" (Companion selling).

Sad isn't it, that some of our salespeople do not regularly step up to the level of the fast food salespeople.

The next level is still reactive but really moves into the sales arena. This is a case where the customer asks for Widget D which we do not have but we do have Widget A which is a cross for Widget D. A salesperson will at least make an attempt to sell them Widget A before resorting to some sort of brokering activity—at best, or telling the customer that we cannot help them (at worst). They will also do the companion sell on Widget D and try to get them to the increase the size of their order. And if you are dealing with a true professional, they will ask how the product will be used, how often it used during the year, other people in the customer location that might use it and permission to call them again at a fixed time to discuss their future needs. Proactive Rating 2

These individuals are at the top of the reactive sales pyramid.

From there, we move to inside salespeople. These people actually initiate sales calls. One of the worst things I ever hear is when I ask how business is and the answer is, "The phones just aren't ringing." A novel idea is to make it ring somewhere else. An inside salesperson will do just that. They will have assigned accounts and work them just like an outside pro and they will try to sell what we want to sell to the people we want to sell to in quantities/put-ups that are good for our business. Proactive Rating 3

From the inside professional, we (theoretically) move to the outside salesperson. A marvel that actually moves to where the customers are and executes sales calls. (Sometimes executes is the right word).

Here, though, it can become really confusing because there are several different types of outside salespeople ranging from route-drivers to sales pros.

Route drivers: Route drivers are the lowest level of outside professional sales. A route driver has a regular list of customers that they visit, often on somewhat consistent schedules. (I think of the snack truck guys or laundry service guys here but that may be unkind because I have met a lot of guys that wear suits and have briefcases that seem to behave the same way). Proactive Rating 4

They can develop low level relationships and this can lead to business. However, as more decisions are made at higher strategic levels, this kind of salesperson's value will decrease. Be advised that some of your salespeople could really be route drivers disguised as salespeople.

Literature fairies (or ferries): A literature fairy/ferry implies one of two things—a salesperson that drops off literature/product information/brochures in the hope that sales will magically spring up where the little seed has been planted. These folks are quite content to be told, "Leave your information at the front desk and I'll look it over."

The derivative of that is the salesperson that thinks that if they can only deliver enough tonnage of literature, they will be successful. Using those definitions, if I come back lighter at the end of the day, I MUST HAVE DONE SOMETHING. For these salespeople, we could just measure the weight of their vehicles on the way out and back in to judge success. Proactive Rating 5

The problem with this approach is that most literature is filed in the county landfill—sooner or later.

Professional visitors: The next level of selling involves people who have only one set of tools in their toolbelt—their good looks, winsome smile and winning personality.

(Those of you that know the author know that this was not an option for him).

These people have relationships—personal relationships and they spend a lot of time developing them. They go from place to place—being likeable. Heaven forbid they ever get forceful enough to ask for an order. Sometimes, these people will tell you they can't push too hard or they'll "ruin the relationship." (The customer in question ordered about $1500 a year and got called on about once a week. Check out the math on that one).
Proactive Rating 6

Outside customer service representatives: This is one of the most insidious problems faced by any sales organization because these people often post good "sales" numbers but they are no longer selling. A long time ago (in a galaxy far, far away), these people were really good salespeople. They were so good that they built a nice book of business.

Now, however, they spend almost all of their time maintaining it. Your company does not really support them so every new order requires them to be intimately involved in the delivery of the product or service. Over time, they still carry a bag and they go out but they are really solving operational problems and maintaining relationships. They have so many transactions that they just cannot proactively sell anymore. Proactive Rating 7

Above these people are the true professionals (note that pro fessional and pro active have the same root (pro). They make real sales calls with real sales objectives and they not only have the literature and the minimum personality skills and the required technical expertise but they also add business value to everything they do. They seek to make things happen. Proactive Rating 8

Despite my (somewhat) negative comments about some of the levels of proactivity expressed above, there is a need for all of them, based on the type of salesperson needed to do the job you need done. The main reason for the categorization is so that you will be able to recognize what you really have and begin to hire more of what you really want.

There are several different types of salespeople and your first decision is what type of salespeople your organization needs. When an organization uses each of these different types of salespeople, it is making an assumption about how the market works. Organizations who have strong customer relationships with growing companies often use route drivers and inside customer service people because that is what is appropriate. Organizations that are trying to get different results from what they previously have obtained normally use the other two proactive kinds of salespeople (inside and outside.)

Don't be fooled by business cards that have the word "Sales" on them. You need to probe and determine how much proactivity they employ during their working day.

Reactive--Proactive

Where are you? Where do you need to be?

Section 4.2 What kinds of salespeople do you really need?

Having gone through all of the issues listed in the previous chapters, you are now ready to put together a picture that describes the kind of salespeople you need to hire from now on. You have already made decisions in the following areas:

Sales strategy
Sales, service or technical support
Geography, market or product segment
Direct, reps or distribution
Inside, outside or both
Formal or random partnerships
Proactive or reactive

You need to think about your answers to all of these questions as you construct a picture of what you want to change about your sales organization as you move forward. If you start with a clear picture, it's easier to get what you want—rather than hire the "best" candidate from a field where "best" is very subjective.

To help you do this more effectively, a chart is provided below as an example. A blank chart is also included in the appendix so that you can thoughtfully fill one out for your organization later.

In the example below, the sales manager has reviewed the strategy and come up with the following picture of what future hires need to look like:

For the outside salesperson, the next hire needs to be someone who has a strong sales aptitude. This is noted by the X in the sales box (twice) and the Proactive Rating of 8. This means that if a strong technical person with a history of heavy account service responsibility comes along, they should not get much consideration.

The sales manager is also looking for an outside salesperson who has previous experience in a geographic territory. So again, if a former product manager or market specialist becomes available, this may not be the right person to hire.

The ideal candidate will also have experience working in a formal partnership with an inside salesperson and will have received most of their compensation from commission, not salary.

These two points may not seem important but they speak volumes about how well a new employee will fit into your system. A person who has never had a formal inside partner might have some difficulty in making the adjustments that you envision. The same is also true of an employee who historically earned most of their income from salary and now is expected to earn the same thing (or hopefully more) on a low salary with a high commission.

For the inside salesperson, the sales manager has indicated a need for a person with a strong service aptitude—note the two Xs in service boxes. The person should have strong product knowledge, however, and some proactive ability—note the 2 rating.

The inside salesperson is also expected to have had previous experience in formal partnering but unlike the outside person, the inside person should have been paid most of their compensation through salary rather than commissions and bonuses.

Category	Outside	Inside
Sales	X	
Technical		
Service		X
Geography	X	
Market		
Product		X
Route driver		
Lit fairy		
Visitor		
Outside CS		
Sales	X	

(chart continued on next page)

Counter		
Service		X
Telesales		
Inside sales		
Proactive Rating	8	2
Formal Partnering	X	X
Random		
Mostly salary		X
Mostly commission	X	

Using this example, you can get a pretty clear picture of what you are looking for when you need to add sales personnel. This not only helps to guide you when you are looking to hire salespeople, it also helps you fight temptation when one of your competitor's salespeople is fired and you think you might want to hire them for all of the mythical business they will bring. (By the way, the statistics say that, on average, they will bring 15% over an 18 month period—so unless they are really what you are looking for, don't hire them).

Once you have decided the type of salespeople you need, you should conduct an assessment of your current people. Did you hire the right kind of people for job you need to do or did you tailor your sales jobs to kinds of people you had?

Section 4.3 Hiring Approaches for Salespeople

Hiring salespeople is one of the most difficult hires that a manager can make. Part of this is because few managers go through the kind of assessment you have just been asked to make concerning the kinds of salespeople that you need. Because of this, a lot of salespeople are hired because it looks like they have had a job like the one they are being offered or because they seem to "fit" the mold, whatever the mold is. Intuition is not an unimportant factor in hiring. A manager's "gut" instinct may be the right one most of the time. And fit is also important. It doesn't matter what kind of credentials a person brings to the job if they cannot adapt to the culture, but there are more systematic ways to hire salespeople and the following are some of the guidelines that help managers to make better hiring decisions.

Create a picture of success. The first step in successful hiring is to create a firm picture of success. When we have made good sales hires in the past what are the measurable characteristics. Do all of the good ones have engineering degrees? (Its OK if some of the bad ones do, too, but what are the characteristics that the good ones share?) Try to stay away from things like, "It felt right," because this is hard to explain to a recruiter and almost impossible to duplicate. What kind of experiences, background, and education do the good ones share?

You're always hiring. A good manager always has their eyes open for potential candidates. Size up the competition's sales force. Size up your supplier's sales force. Pay attention to the intern that hangs around the sales office and volunteers to make calls. You are always looking for people that have the success characteristics.

They're easier to make than to hire. You're going to hate this one but often you really can't teach an old dog new tricks. Especially if you're in an industry where sales has always meant "customer service" and you want it to mean "sales." Managers often make the mistake of trying to hire a veteran salesperson under the mistaken impression that they will not have to train them. Even a veteran needs to be trained on how you do it. And years of doing it some other way may be harder to break than teaching it right the first time.

Have a formal integration plan. If a hire is worth making, it's worth doing right. This means having a formal plan for what you expect of people by specified milestones, for instance 30, 60 and 90 days. Set activity targets (not results targets) for those milestones and hold people accountable for doing them. If they fail at the activities, most of the time they ultimately fail at the results.

Hire based on your plan. I know that you can get this great guy from the competition but is it really what you want? And that guy who just doesn't fit anywhere else in the organization thinks he might want a job in sales, but do you want him? Don't be railroaded into hiring someone who does not fit with what you need to accomplish your goals.

The Hiring Process

Most of this you've heard before but it bears repeating. Have a formal process for hiring people. If you have a repeatable process, you can begin to make corrections based on the results you are getting. If every hire is different, you can't learn any lessons from it.

All hiring processes should include the following:

Ask for resumes. Use them to eliminate time-wasters. Review them and compare their answers to some of the items presented below and screen out those that do not appear to fit what you want.

Ask them to submit something in writing that is not their resume. Most really effective salespeople are good communicators. This means that they can write a coherent sentence. Ask them to submit an essay (500 words) on why they want to work for your company. If that puts them off, they will never get through the myriad of hurdles that customers put them through and it would be good to see how they write about something other than themselves.

Have multiple interviews. Don't hire someone unless you have interviewed them twice—no matter how great that first interview went.

Have multiple interviewees. Always have multiple people assist you in the interviews—maybe even one of your salespeople. Who says it has to be a manager? Even non-sales managers can provide insight. Put them through a gauntlet and let them try and sell multiple people in your organization. Won't they need that skill to succeed in your business?

The Selection Process

Selecting the right person has an element of art and a strong dose of science or process. The issues listed below will help you to create a formal process. Rate the applicant from a 1-10 in each of the areas (1 being terrible and 10 being perfect.)

Review the resume and look for a lot of job changes. If the person averages less than two years per job, they are probably not a good hire. You want someone to who has some level of dedication to a job because many sales jobs are not rewarding until you have worked a year or two. (This is not true if you are interviewing anyone under 27 who may have had two or three jobs in quick succession when they left school. Sometimes it takes them a while to figure out that reality is not like what they may have been told.)

Look for the type of work experience you want—not necessarily the technical background. A good inside salesperson can learn about the nuances of your business. A customer service rep may not be able to make the transition to inside salesperson— regardless of their technical competence in your field. Specifically, see if they meet the criteria you spelled out for a good hire on your chart.

Ask to review their calendars. If they are currently in a sales job, they should have one and should be willing to show it to you. If it is a competitor, give them a confidentiality agreement that you will not use the data you see. You are looking for evidence that they are professionals not the names of customers.

Look for some of the following:

Professionals have appointments.

Professionals have appointments scheduled before 9:00 and after 3:30.

Professionals do not have more than one half-day block with no appointments scheduled.

Professionals even have calls on Monday mornings and Friday afternoons.

<u>This applies even to inside salespeople who should have some appointments.</u>

Look for people who have a desire to sell. Ask questions about where they want to be, career-wise, in three to five years. People that tell you that they will have been made a manager in your organization within the first two years probably will not work out—unless you are making this hire with the desire to find a manager.

Ask them what they will be earning in three to five years. If the figure is reasonable, they will make a good candidate. If the figure is too high for the job you are offering ($175,000, for instance) or too low ($27,500, for example), you should be wary of hiring them. The first number indicates someone who either is out of touch with your industry and will be very disappointed very quickly and the second number indicates someone who will settle for mediocrity.

Ask them how they feel about quotas/goals. A professional will have no problem with the accountability that comes from goals. Others will not feel good about them.

Listen for references to "team" selling. Most of the time persons interviewing for sales positions that want to be a member of a "team" are really saying that they want to avoid individual responsibility. Listen carefully for statements that sound like that and explore the issue fully.

Ask them about life goals. Most successful salespeople have clear life goals. The less the person you are dealing with understands about what they want out of life the less likely they are to succeed at selling which requires a lot of self-direction.

Ask them to sell you something. Set up an opportunity during the interview for them to sell you something. Even if they have never sold before, ask them to sell you something they know about. Listen to their approach. Do they try to sell value or quickly cut price? What kind of salesperson do you want?

Ask them the reason they are leaving their current job. People tend to leave if they are dissatisified. Find out what dissatisified them. If the reason is that their commission was cut when they started making good money, you may have a good candidate because this is a valid reason. If the candidate cannot give you a reason or if they give you a poor justification such as the fact that their previous boss did not like them—watch out.

A casual observer would notice that there are 10 questions. If you routinely use this, you will begin to see what candidates work out the best. You would assume that the higher scores would be the best hires and this is often the case but not always. Some organizations find that the individuals that score between 70 and 80 are the best hires, long term. Applicants who score very high may simply be using your job as a stepping stone. Pay attention to the

Joseph C. Ellers

scores you give and hire the people that fall within the success ratio.

Regardless of how you feel about a candidate, a score of 50 or less is almost always the kiss of death.

Sales Management Self-Audit

Rate each answer on a scale of 1-14 with 1 being "Not at all" and 14 being "Totally."

_____We have a defined sales focus: proactive versus reactive.

_____We have a documented picture of the salespeople we need.

_____We have an on-going formal recruitment strategy.

_____We have a formal integration plan that supports the new hire.

_____We hire based on our plan.

_____We have a formal hiring process which we follow every time.

_____We have a formal selection process which we follow every time.

Add your numbers and give yourself a score: _____. (Add back the 2 points I took away from you in the scoring process for being a model student, again.)

Section 5.0 Sales Planning

For many managers, a vague feeling of uneasiness settles over them as they put together sales plans for the upcoming year. The scenario is often the same:

The company gives them a number; they give it to the sales team. The sales team either says they can't do it—or worse they say they can and then don't.

By the end of the first quarter, some salespeople are ahead; others are behind. There are always reasons, good reasons, why this is so. Acme pushed a big order out. Ajax pulled a big order in. But somehow it was wrong because the salespeople should have known those accounts well enough to have known about some of those things at least.

The worst part is that even the budgets that were on target at the top line were often off in other places. The total sales number was all right but it wasn't coming from the right things. The two new products they needed to sell were down while some products they were de-emphasizing made up for all of the growth.

The same was true with customers. Management had picked five new accounts they said they wanted to open up during the year. The sales team only had orders from two of them and they were insignificant.

And the worst part is that the manager really doesn't know what to do about it.

This scenario has its roots in the sales planning process. The good news is that you can make it better.

Section 5.1 Overview

The desire to focus on numbers as the approach to sales planning is almost universal. Because sales results are quantifiable, most sales planning is done with numbers. And because many organizations (correctly) tend not to believe salespeople's input, the process is often arbitrary.

If the goal is to create a real sales plan for the organization, it will have several specific features:

A formal process that gathers input from the salespeople
A planning calendar that is on-going and constant
A strategic sales planning matrix that drives activities
A formal follow-up method which completes the circle

The final result of a sales plan should be a set of numbers that everyone can count on and where everyone is in agreement. If you create a plan that either management or the sales team disagrees with, there is a problem. Have there been times when both disagreed?

Section 5.2 Process/Planning Calendar

For some reason, many sales managers do not do a thorough job of annual sales planning. Or at best, the job goes something like this—the manager meets with the salespeople and they through an exercise where the salesperson tries to low ball expectations and the manager sets targets that are not attainable because they are willing to accept a lower number anyway.

Effective sales management includes an element of effective sales planning and there is a process that you should follow:

<u>Quarterly Reviews (Month 3, 6)</u>

Sales planning for next years begins at the end of the first quarter of this year. At the end of every quarter, you need to do a quick review to ensure that there is some correlation between the results and the plan. Most managers will find that some salespeople are close to the plan and others are no where near it. While we acknowledge that being behind plan is a problem, being dramatically ahead of plan is also a problem—although a nicer problem to have.

You want to be able to count on your plan and this means being accurate. In most instances, there is always an attempt to rationalize why we are behind plan (Acme pushed out a big order) or ahead of plan (Acme pulled in a big order), but often we do not use the delta as a learning experience. What were the factors that the salesperson could have noticed that would have made the plan more realistic? Your goal is to look at the salesperson's ability to deliver to plan on a quarterly basis (for planning purposes) and see what it tells you about putting together next year's plan.

Beginning of Quarter 4 (Month 9)

Sales planning begins in earnest at the start of Q4. By that time you will have ¾ of the current year under your belt and you will have a pretty good idea how the current year will finish up. At this point, you need to need to be reviewing the strategic plan. Where does the business need to be over the next two to three years? What different results are needed over the next 12 months? Are there new products or services that need to be introduced? New market segments that need to be explored? Are any major product lines in jeopardy? Are any major customers in jeopardy?

Month 10

At the beginning of the 10th month, you be finalizing the tentative company budget. It can be tweaked but you should have an understanding of what you need to do by the end of this month.

Month 11

	Existing products/services	New products/services
Existing customers	$10 million	$2 million
New customers	$2 million	$500,000

During this month, you have a lot to do. The first step is to construct a company 3 x 3. You remember this document from the first section. Then you need to construct tentative 3 x 3s for each of your sales territories.

Each territory will probably lose some business. Based on the historic loss of business and the conditions that exist in each territory, are your Box 1 numbers realistic? Will some territories be effected more than others?

How likely is it that the salespeople will have the time required to open up new customers? Some of your salespeople might be tied down servicing existing customers and have limited time to do prospecting activities. How much time can you reasonably expect each salesperson to spend on these activities?

How well positioned are we to do the new product or service introductions that you have tentatively outlined? A territory may have a lot of potential but the salesperson may have limited product knowledge. Is there a learning curve that has to be considered?

You want to do your own reality check. And, now that you have constructed these 3 x 3s, put them aside for a while.

Your next step is to give blank 3 x 3 documents to each of your salespeople and ask them to do a high level forecast for their territories. An important aspect of this forecast is to tell them that it is **not** going to be their budget but it will be used to help establish their budget. If they think that the numbers they submit will be accepted fully or rejected fully, they will submit a different set of numbers than you want. You want them to tell you what they think they really can do. (You need to save these forecasts for comparison, by the way, especially if the budget you agree on is significantly different. You will look at these forecasts as part of your quarterly review and compare it to the actual budget to see who had a better understanding of their territory—them or you).

You need their forecasts to be completed by the end of month 11. This will give you time to compare what you get back with what you estimated and what you need to accomplish your goals. It will also give you the time you need to negotiate a final set of numbers with your salespeople.

A real negotiation is critical. If they think they can do $2.2 million and you assign a goal of $3 million, you have probably doomed the process. The purpose of the negotiation is to uncover reasons why the salesperson thinks that cannot do a number and then to work with them to eliminate the problem but if you arbitrarily give them a number, you are really taking them off the hook for making it. (The same holds true when a too optimistic number is submitted—especially when 50% of the projected sales come in the 4th quarter—the old hockey stick forecast.)

At this point, you can stop because you have a budget but there is one additional tool that I would strongly recommend because it will not only make planning more effective but it will make it easier to manage sales during the course of the year:

The tool is a sales planning matrix.

Section 5.3 Sales Strategic Planning Matrix

If you have done your job correctly, you have established company-wide sales goals using the 3 x 3 matrix. You have then negotiated sales goals with the sales team, using the same 3 x 3 as an overview that will address the following:

Sales of existing products to existing customers
Sales of new products to existing customers
Sales of existing products to new customers
Sales of new products to new customers

The next level of sales planning is to take this one step further and construct a Sales Strategic Planning Matrix for each sales territory. A sample is provided below:

	Product A	Product B	Service C	Product D
Customer 1	12,000/14,000	5000/5000	2500/5000	0/5000
Customer 2	0/10,000	5000/7000	1000/?	0/?
Prospect 3	0/10,000	0/5000	0/?	0/?
Customer 4	0/?	0/0	500/15,000	5000/5000

Remember from earlier discussions that you were asked to prioritize the things that your company wanted to sell. In the example above, the products and services that we want to sell are presented from left to right across the top of the chart with Product A being most important and Product D being the least important item presented. The maximum number of focus items would be 10 and these need to be the same for everyone in the organization. The point is not to do a different list for every territory but to do a consistent

81

list. (If there are wide disparities between the kinds of opportunities in different territories, you will handle this through the budget process.)

You need to note that these are not necessarily presented in order of sales volume. Product A could have 0$ in sales but it still might be the most important thing for the sales force to focus on during the coming year.

The same holds true for the customers/prospects that are presented (in descending order of importance) down the side of the chart. Again, Customer 1 might not be the customer the salesperson did the most volume with last year. And notice that a prospect ranks higher than some existing customers. The maximum number of customers/prospects for this list would be 25. (With 10 focus sales items, this would give each salesperson a maximum of 250 different boxes to concentrate on.) If your organization is like most, this will capture about 80% of the sales (or potential) for the territory.

This exercise has two goals: to establish priority in the minds of the salespeople and to drive daily activities. Everyone in the sales staff would be very clear on both of these points if you presented them with this chart.

With the priorities firmly established, the next step is to put the sales for the previous year in each box. So in the example presented, the salesperson sold $12,000 worth of Product A at Customer 1 last year.

Now comes the hard part. In our example, you see that there are either two numbers or a (?). The tough assignment is for the salesperson to put the estimated potential for the upcoming year in each of the boxes. Again, using our example, the salesperson estimated that the potential for Product A at Customer 1 in the upcoming year is $14,000. Sounds simple, and it is, if the salesperson understands the account.

As you can see, this process drives a lot of the right kind of sales behaviors. First, it serves as a rock-solid planning document that makes your job (and theirs) a lot easier during the year. The second purpose, is that it drives the right kind of sales knowledge. If a salesperson knows enough about an account to understand its potential, they are likely to have a better chance of selling that account.

If you have never done this kind of exercise before, it will be accomplished with much wailing, moaning and gnashing of teeth. This is especially true because many salespeople (not yours, I know) have a habit of estimating that they are getting all of the business in a great many of their accounts. This is true in some cases but not nearly as many as we might think.

A major caveat here is that, as sales manager, you must have some understanding of potential. If there is a correlation between the customer's total sales and the use of your products, you have to know it. If there is a correlation between the use of Product A and Product B, you have to know it. You need to have some guidelines that give you some insight into the account. If for instance, they are a chemical manufacturer with 400 employees and your salesperson tells you that they purchase only $100,000 a year of raw materials, you have to know enough to argue the point.

Once the salesperson has estimated potential, the sales plan becomes a piece of cake because, we are now faced with a group of boxes and for each of those boxes, at any given, time there is only one of five strategies that can be employed. This is where we begin to translate the numbers into activities.

Defend
Introduce
Grow
Find Out
Forget About

Defend. Let's take them one at a time. Look at Box B1. The salesperson estimates that they have all of the possible sales. If you agree with this (and you're skeptical), there is only one thing to be done in this box over the course of the year—Defend it. As a manager, you need to spend some time discussing the appropriate defense strategies for that account. Do we need to identify more of the influencers in the account that use product? Provide more technical support? Lock up the order in an annual agreement? Whatever you decide, both you and the salesperson are in agreement about that box.

Introduce. The second possibility is illustrated in Box A2. We are currently getting $0 (hard to believe, isn't it?) but the salesperson has estimated that they will use $10,000 worth of the product over the coming year. The strategy here is to Introduce our product into this account. You need to work with the salesperson to decide the tactics to do this. For example, do we need to get one of our technical people in there? Identify the decision-maker?

And you also need to agree on what qualifies as "Introduce." The sale of a sample order? An order for $500? Once this is accomplished, you can then consider moving on to the next step.

Grow. Growth implies that you are already getting some portion of the business. Box C4 appears to provide the biggest opportunity here. We are currently getting $500 and there is $15,000 worth of potential. Again, you need to set a realistic growth target and discuss what they intend to do to accomplish this strategy. "I'm gonna be all over them this year," is not really a strategy. Finding decision-makers, making presentations, giving them samples, bringing in technical support people are all growth **activities.**

Find out. In the first year of this process, you will be directing a lot of "Find out" activities because you may not even agree with some of the estimates of potential that are presented. Boxes A4 and C2 are different examples of this. In A2, the salesperson is getting no business. Is this because there is no potential? We need to "Find Out." In C2, we've got sales but we do not know if we have all of it or not or if they intend to purchase any of it this year, so again, we have to "Find Out." Sometimes you can get this information by asking. Sometimes, you have to connect the usage of this service or product to something else they do. But you do not know how much effort to put in either of these boxes until you answer this question.

Forget about. You cannot sell what they are not buying and Box B4 is a good example of this. They purchased $0 and their estimated potential is $0 so we Forget About it—for now, at least. (Be careful about this one. Sometimes, they are buying a competitive product and the salesperson thinks that because they bought $0 there is $0 potential. Explore this $0 carefully).

Once you have gone through this exercise, you will have a great sales plan that not only helps you manage the big picture but also provides you with a great follow-up tool that will allow you to drive tactics during the year.

Section 5.4 Sales Follow-up Applications

Once you have established this sort of sales plan, you have also simplified your sales management for the coming year. You are no longer in the position of telling salespeople to "get out there and sell something" because the two of you have agreed on exactly what they need to do in each of their key accounts. Obviously, this may not cover everything they need to do but it ought to cover the lion's share of focus activities.

	Product A	Product B	Service C	Product D
Customer 1	12,000/14,000	5000/5000	2500/5000	0/5000
Customer 2	0/10,000	5000/7000	1000/?	0/?
Prospect 3	0/10,000	0/5000	0/?	0/?
Customer 4	0/?	0/0	500/15,000	5000/5000

The matrix also has five very specific on-going sales management uses:

Pre-call planning
Opportunity management
Problem identification
Training
Forecasting

Pre-call planning. If you ask for itineraries (which we will discuss later), you should compare the proposed schedule of the salesperson with the planning matrix. If, for example, the salesperson with the above plan has a week worth of calls planned and none of them seem to address any of the items highlighted in the matrix, this might be a problem. If it occurs two weeks in a row, it is definitely a problem and you have the ability to do something about it.

A second use would be as a preparation aid in advance of a specific sales call. If you were reviewing a planned sales call on Customer 1 above, the action items are pretty simple:

Grow (maybe) Box A1
Defend Box B1
Grow Box C1
Introduce Box D1

Rather than a generic discussion about what they intend to do, you could review some very specific issues around the strategies outlined above.

Opportunity Management. Another topic that I will spend some time on later is opportunity management. At this point, simply consider how the plan above would aid you in tracking of opportunities. If you expect sales of Product D, you would expect to see presentations, samples and quotes for Product D in Customer 1. This would allow you to quickly check to see if progress was being made in the areas where you both agreed that progress would be made.

Problem identification. This logically allows you to identify problems before they become acute. Remember our sales manager who was having difficulty not only because the numbers were off but also off in areas of importance. By planning at this level, the sales manager can see very early in the year how efforts are progressing in focus areas—focus products and customers. If the right activities are not taking place early in the year, the odds are that the right results will not follow.

Training/development. Many managers who use this system also find value in reviewing it to develop their training and development plans for the year. There are two ways to read this chart—from top to bottom in a given column and from left to right in a given row.

A good example of how this would apply would be to review the D column. If you look at this, the salesperson has 0$ sales in the top three accounts in the territory and only $5,000 in the fourth. The most interesting thing, from the view of sales management, would be the lack of understanding of potential in two of the accounts. If you look at the territory this way, you get the feeling that this salesperson does not necessarily know enough about this product to sell it effectively. This, then, suggests a training need. If the sales manager noticed a similar trend in multiple salespeople the need might be general and the manger might structure a specific training program just to address this issue.

The other way to read this data is from left to right and we can use Customer 4 as the example. This is obviously an important customer but the salesperson has very low sales dollars in the top four products/services. Further, the salesperson does not even know the potential for the most important product (A) at that customer. This might suggest a lack of understanding of the account. If similar accounts had similar results, there might be a more general problem with this salesperson. If the problem occurred on similar accounts covered by other salespeople, again, there might be an opportunity for a general training program aimed at helping salespeople to understand this particular type of account better.

Forecasting. The final way in which this may be used in on-going sales management is in forecasting and planning. If a salesperson really understands their key accounts at this level, they will be much better able to forecast future revenues. Think about how easy it would be for them, next year, when they are asked to forecast if they have this document in front of them. Also, consider how easy it will be for you to plan if you have this data.

Sales Management Self-Audit

Rate each answer on a scale of 1-16 with 1 being "Not at all" and 16 being "Totally."

_____We have a defined sales planning process.
_____We have a formal process for gathering input from our salespeople.
_____We have a negotiated approach where we get real agreement on sales plans.
_____We have a formal planning calendar.
_____Our planning process drives specific activities.
_____Our planning process allows for easy sales management follow-up.

Add your numbers and give yourself a score: _____. (Add back the 4 points I took away from you in the scoring process. I am mellowing with age.)

Section 6.0 Sales Process

After addressing the necessary prerequisites, we are now to the crux of the book: managing the sales <u>process</u>. Note the emphasis on process. While there are artistic components in selling, your goal as a sales manager is to help your salespeople to understand that selling is a process that can be monitored, measured and managed. In my consulting, I have worked with hundreds of organizations. Running through every sales situation there are specific activities that need to be done everytime. We have presented these activities in an easy-to-follow format that will cover most of the sales situations that you run into. (There will be exceptions, of course, but you want to focus on the rules. After all, not every bear you encounter in the woods will attack you, but you steer clear of all of them, anyway.)

The same is true of selling—you might need to modify the process to better suit your business, but the basic framework holds true for every business-to-business sale we have witnessed. There are multiple advantages to a sales manager who applies a formal process to the sales function. The most important is that it allows you to focus on the "real" issues. Most sales managers look at the results (orders booked) and make assumptions about how effective salespeople are. This is one starting place but not necessarily the real answer.

Some salespeople have good territories, good customers, good inside support people-and good luck.

Other people may be better salespeople but missing some of the ingredients listed above. To maximize your effectiveness, you need some formal systems that allow you to diagnose where the real sales problems are.

Most sales managers tend to look at a low level of sales and immediately assume that the problem is closing ability. In fact, for years most sales training efforts focused on the close. But this might not be the real problem-in fact, most often, it isn't. Think about two basketball players: Player A takes 15 shots a game and scores 10 points. Player B takes 3 shots a game and scores 4 points. Who looks better on the results side? Who looks better on the effectiveness side?

Player A has 250% more "sales" than Player B but Player B has a "closing" percentage twice as good as Player A. We really have two sales management problems here:Player A needs to "close" more sales and Player B needs to take more shots. But if you just look at the results, A looks like a better player.

The final key value in managing a "process" is that it makes the salesperson more effective. If you were to ask any of your salespeople what step of the sales process they are in for each major opportunity, what they need to accomplish to move it to the next step and what the next step is—what kind of answers would you get?

For you to manage (and intervene,) in advance, in critical sales efforts, you need to teach your people a process. You are teaching them a language that applies to sales. This language is a shortcut that allows you to get to the heart of any sales matter. Rather than asking how a particular opportunity is going—and listening to a rambling dissertation, you can simply ask what stage of the sale they are in, ask a few penetrating questions and sit back and let the brilliance of their answers wash over you like a waterfall.

That is why you will find the six step process presented below to be a valuable sales management tool. I have broken the sale into its definable steps and tried to capture the essence of what has to happen at each step.

You also need to keep the following in mind as you review the steps:

A sale can be in only one step at any given time. You can't be qualifying a customer and quoting a piece of business at the same time. You're always at the earliest part of the sale that you have not completed— because if you have not completed part of the process you will either have to repeat it—or worse, not make the sale.

Each step has some activities that must take place to allow it to move to the next step. Whether we realize it or not, our customers often do a lot of the work for us. We have all been trying to sell something and had a customer ask, "Where do I sign?" or "When can we get started?" This is an example of the customer closing themselves—and they do other part so the sale for us. But a professional salesperson makes sure that each step is done before moving on and this is one of the things that separates the great ones from the average ones.

Finally, I have a visceral hatred of "Maybes" everywhere in life but especially in sales. A "Maybe" answer is tough because I just don't know what to do with a "Maybe" and unfortunately a huge percentage of "Maybes" turn out to be "Nos" in the final analysis. To be effective, a sales process has to focus on Yes/No answers. A "Maybe" is a timewaster and you need a process that will help identify reality. By using the process we describe, you will help your salespeople to uncover problems earlier because you will focus them on getting "Yes" and "No" answers—rather than "Maybes." This will not only eliminate a lot of garbage from their days but help them to increase their sales.

Section 6.1 Overview

In our work, we have identified six specific steps that a sale goes through. (Note that I am not advocating a "canned" process where the salespeople go through a series of scripted questions and statements. Although there are situations where that might be the best approach.) Instead, I am talking about a series of phases that are distinct enough to be identified.

Step 1. Customer Identification/Qualification. The first part of any sale is to try and find an organization that can (ability) and will (desire) buy what you are selling. To use an old sales term, this is part of the "prospecting" process. For most sales managers, this means identifying organizations that buy and can afford the products or services that you want to sell. If you have all the customers you want, skip on to the next step.

Step 2. Decision-Making Process (DMP) Identification/Qualification. The second part of any sale is finding the right people inside the customer (or prospect) organization. Opportunities are controlled by people. Purchasing decisions are made by people. The second half of the prospecting process is to identify all of the people who can help the salesperson to make a sale. Again, if your sales team has already done this with all of the customers you will ever need, skip on to the next step.

Step 3. Opportunity Identification/Qualification. Of all of the steps in sales, this (not closing) is the one where most sales failures occur. This is the step where the salesperson finds a piece of business that they have a chance of selling. Most of the time when we fail to sell, it's not price or features or service but the simple fact that the customer really did not a reason to start doing business with us—there was no "real" opportunity.

Step 4. Evaluation/Qualification (by the Prospect/Customer.) Most salespeople put this step before Step 3 in the mistaken belief that if the customer approves their organization, product or service, an opportunity will be created. (You can be on the Approved Vendor List and still never get orders but more about that later.) This is the step where the customer answers the question, "Will this proposed solution work in my application?" Some organizations do this step very formally and others do it informally but it must be done.

Step 5. Quotes and Proposals. If all of the previous steps have been done correctly, the sale moves to some sort of quote or proposal. These can be verbal or very formal but again, it has to be done. The problem is that a great many sales organizations think the sales process begins here. The only real quotes occur after the first four steps are done and your organization needs to understand the "real" quotes when they see them.

Step 6. Closing. If all of the previous steps have been done correctly, the final stage of the sale is the close. This is where we get the prospect or customer's commitment.

We will address each step separately and provide insight on what needs to happen and things you can do as a manager to make it work better. But before we do, you need an overview of the customer's buying processes.

Section 6.2 Customer's Buying Process

From a salesperson's point of view, the sale has the six steps described previously. From the customer's point of view, they look at the process differently. For the purpose of this discussion, we will describe the steps that the customer goes through so that you can see how they mesh with the sales process. This will also tie in neatly to a previous section dealing with creating our value proposition and deciding where to compete.

Think of each sale as a timeline. It starts at some point with an organization that has a need or an opportunity and it ends in an order. (We are going to ignore all the things that happen after the order for the purposes of this discussion.) The sales process can take seconds (as in the case where a customer reorders something they have ordered before) or it can take years (if you are working on a piece of major capital equipment or a facilities expansion.)

The Customer's Process

The customer's process has the following steps:

Trigger
Design
Transition
Purchasing
Order

Trigger: The first step in the customer's process begins when a decision is made that requires them to buy something. This might be the decision to build a new product, reduce cost in an existing product, expand their facility, sub out some part of their workforce or whatever. It could also be something simple like something breaking. No matter what you sell, there is a reason why there is a need for it and this need is the beginning of an opportunity. Many times the people involved in this process are very high in the organization—and often they make decisions that our contacts are unaware of unless our sales force is directed to interact with them. Many organizations completely ignore this part of the process but some organizations are involved in it. (An example of this would be an electronics salesperson who presents their new product to a Vice President of a computer company in hopes that the VP will mandate a redesign of their product to include the salesperson's component.)

Design: Once a decision has been made that something is needed, the customer then decides what "it" is. This may be a long process where they interview fifteen different engineering firms before deciding which one to hire for a plant expansion or it could be as simple as looking up an item on the Approved Vendor list. But in each case, the customer had to decide "What" it needed. Many times, technical people are involved in this decision, but not always.

Transition: The transition process involves how the need for something moves from whatever part of the organization needs it into the purchasing process. This involves requisitions and specification (reqs and specs) in larger organizations and an exchange between two people in the break area in small ones. (This will be discussed in more detail in Section 6.4.)

Purchasing: This part of the process is focused on answering the question of "Who", as in Who will buy it from? Once the professional purchasing people get a request, they do something. Sometimes, a whole lot of somethings. They might evaluate the supplier's organization or product/service. They might organize a formal bid process. The important aspect from a sales perspective is to understand what happens.

Order: When a decision has been made to buy something from someone, the organization orders it. Sometimes this is done by people that have decision-making authority and sometimes not. But it is the last part of the customer's process.

To help understand how this works, look at the examples below.

Example 1: A maintenance employee is using a drill. The drill breaks (Trigger.) The employee decides that he needs the exact same drill (Design.) He calls purchasing (Transition) and asks for a new drill. The purchasing employee looks up the part number, sees that three suppliers are qualified to sell it, calls all three and asks them for a quote (Purchasing.) The purchasing employee then places an order with their preferred supplier (Order.)

Example 2: The management team decides that they need to re-engineer their plant floor to improve throughput efficiency by 15% (Trigger). A team of industrial engineers is tasked with coming up with a plan. They meet and develop a tentative set of specifications. Then they call in a series of potential vendors including architects, engineering consultants, equipment vendors and construction companies. Based on their reviews, they develop a set of specifications. (Design) These specifications are transmitted to purchasing (Transition). The purchasing department then stages a formal bid process—inviting only the organizations that have been approved by engineering. They review the submissions and determine who both meets the specifications and the target prices supplied by the industrial engineering group. They then select the vendors that will be participating in the project (Purchasing). A clerk in the department then issues the purchase orders (Order.)

In both of these instances, the process is followed but in the second example, the process is significantly more complex.

The diagram presented below shows how the customer's processes affect the sales process:

Design versus Purchase

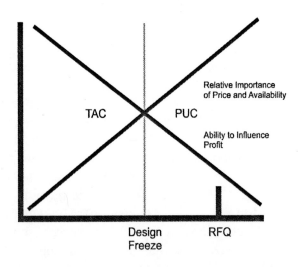

The vertical line represents the trigger point or the point at which any specific opportunity starts. The horizontal line is a timeline. This line can take 6 minutes (Example 1) or 24 months (Example 2.) The end of the horizontal line is the point at which the purchase order is issued to the supplier.

Note that there are two slanting lines that intersect. These lines are key because they not only provide insight into the relative effectiveness of various parts of the sales process, but they also show how the world works.

We'll begin with Line A which is defined as the Ability to Influence line. This line documents the ability of the selling organization to influence the outcome of any sales opportunity. Most would agree that if we write the specs, for instance, we have a much greater ability to influence the outcome than if we find out about it when the customer goes out for bids.

Line B demonstrates the relative importance of Price and Availability in the customer's buying decision. Late in the process, the customer normally wants to be able to get it quickly and if more than one organization can supply it, they want it from the cheapest source.

The intersection of these lines cuts the customer's process into two parts. On the left hand side are the Trigger and the Design process. On the right hand side are the Purchasing Process and the Order. The dotted line in the middle represents the Transition or the Design Freeze Point.

TAC versus PUC

The Transition point is critical when thinking about your sales strategy because it serves as the dividing line between the customer processes that focus on

Total Acquisition Cost (TAC) and Per Unit Cost (PUC—pronounced puke, not puck.)

When your salespeople are involved in the TAC portion (Trigger/Design), there are a lot of factors that might help them get the sale. (A sample list was provided in Section 2.)

As the customer's process moves to the right along the line, less factors are important. After you cross the Transition line, PUC (Purchasing/Order) begins to gain the upper hand and at the Order level, there are really only two questions:

Can you give it to the customer when they need it? (Availability)

Is your price the cheapest? (Price)

As a sales organization, you can focus most of your efforts in one of the four areas:

Trigger
Design
Purchasing
Order

Trigger: Some sales organizations invest heavily in making calls at the very beginning of the process. Their goal is to help create the need or to be there when the need is created. An example of this would be an industrial equipment salesperson who calls on the VP of Manufacturing to convince them to redesign their plant floor to reduce waste by purchasing the salesperson's equipment.

Design: Some sales organizations wait until the decision has been made to do something and then try to influence it at the design stage. An example would be an electronic components salesperson who tries to get their part designed into the new personal computer.

Purchasing: Another sales approach is to wait until the request comes to purchasing and then to try to win the business there based on service and relationship. An example would be an industrial salesperson who knows that they buy abrasives and waits until the requisition hits purchasing before trying to win the business.

Order: Many catalog organizations simply wait until an order is about to be placed. They win business because they have it in stock or because they are the cheapest.

A key decision for sales management is: How do I want to focus my sales effort?

Remember the earlier discussions on strategy. Once you understand where you want your salespeople to spend most of their time, you can use the six step sales process to ensure that they are doing the right things with the right people at the right times.

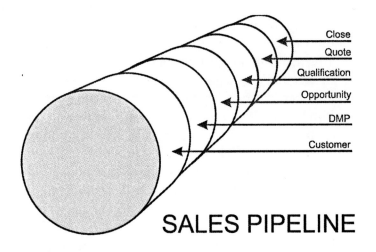

SALES PIPELINE

Section 6.3 Identifying/Qualifying the prospect (Step 1)

The first step in the sales process is to find and qualify potential customers. Assuming that we are talking about professional selling, we are talking about first identifying organizations (not individuals), then ensuring that they are qualified to buy what we are selling. This is only true if your organization has a goal to find new customers over the next year.

So, sales manager, answer the question, based on your strategy, do we need new customers?

If the answer is "yes," then you need to have a formal process for identification and qualification. This means that there are several specific activities that salespeople should do and several sales management tools that can help you help them to do them.

You also have to make one other key decision, on a territory-by-territory basis:

How much sales time do you want spent on prospecting activities? 10% (20+ days per year)? 30% (60+ days per year)? You have to answer this question for each territory before each new year begins.

Sales Activities

If you refer to your answers to the strategic questions, you have already identified the kind of new business you want. (Remember your answers to the questions: What do you want to sell? Who do you want to sell it to? And, what does a good order look like?)

You want prospecting activities to be directed finding the kind of customers you want that can buy the kind of products/services you want to sell in orders that you want to receive. You might not get all three but this is what you want.

Target Customer List

If this is your goal, you need to begin with a formal target customer list for each sales territory. After reviewing the 3 x 3 matrix with your salesperson, ask them to put together a list of prospects that "appear" to meet the criteria. The number of prospects on the list will be related to the amount of time that you want the salesperson to spend on prospecting. As an example, if you have a veteran salesperson who is currently doing $4-5 million in sales, you might have one or two names only on the list-because you want them to spend 5% or less of their time on prospecting. A brand new salesperson, however, might have 50 names on the list because you might want them to spend most of their time working the list.

Once they have put the list together, you need to review it with them and discuss why they put the prospect on the list. Based on what they can tell you, do they seem to be kind of business you want? Why or why not?

As a manager you should give them feedback on this effort because if you just accept the list, you might be letting them waste a lot of time. So if you know that Customer ABC is a lousy credit risk, maybe you should tell them to put that one at the bottom of the list (or not on the list at all). Remember, too, that the focus prospect names should also be on the Sales Strategic Planning Matrix See section 5.3.

If you are doing your job well, you will review the list on a monthly basis-as part of your on-going management activities. Some names will be dropped because they do not pass muster. Other names will be added. If you need a significant portion of your business to come from new customers, this list will be included in almost every sales discussion.

Survey Activities and Profiles

With the list in hand, many salespeople want to skip a few key activities. They want to make appointments and try to sell the people on their prospect list. Sounds reasonable, you might be thinking, but many times, it's not the next step.

A reasonable next step involves two sales (and sales management) tools-survey activities and customer profiles.

The salespeople have put together a list, a hypothesis, really, that a group of prospects meet our definition of "good." Rather than run out and start selling them, they should test this hypothesis. They do this by doing surveying activities (including survey calls) and a good account profile can guide them.

There are many surveying activities:

Researching the company on the Internet
Reading articles about them in the local papers
Asking other (non-competitive) suppliers about them
Facility tours

Your salespeople need to do some (all) of these activities before trying to sell anything.

The second half of the question, however, is the most important. What are they looking for with their surveying activities?

As a manager, you want to lay out some specific pieces of data that you want them to find. As a starting point, I would like to recommend the following:

Company size: (Sales, employees, square footage) or any other number that provides a checkpoint for potential. This will also help to validate the hypothesis that this is a prospect that meets our definition of "good."

Potential: What is their estimate of sales potential for the products you want to sell? There is no way to over-emphasize the importance of this piece of information. All decisions about how much time (and organizational resource) should be devoted to a particular customer flow from this piece of knowledge. If they purchase $1 million worth of your product, you would probably spend more time with them than if they purchase $10,000.

As a manager, you also need to develop some key indicators that give you a check on the information you get when you ask the salesperson this question. In some industries, your potential is a percentage of their total sales or connected to the square footage of their facility or some other fairly obtainable piece of information.

You want to know enough so that when a salesperson tells you that a prospect does $50 million worth of business at a facility and they are running two shifts with 200 employees on each shift that they cannot be only buying $10,000 of your product, regardless of what the purchasing agent just told your salesperson.

Decision-making authority: How are decisions made to purchase what you want to sell?

List of contacts/job titles: We want to know who the salesperson has identified. Have they only found low level people? Do they know enough people? The right people? (More about this in Step 2, as well.)

Customer's goals: What is the customer trying to accomplish this year? Does this match up with any of our strengths? Can we have competitive advantage, other than price?

Fiscal year/budget process: If this is relevant, how does it work within their organization?

What other big picture questions do you want them to find out, before they begin to try and book an order? (You will use this information to flesh out an Account Profile.)

The goal is to understand if this organization is a "real" prospect. Do they buy what we want to sell? Are the decision-makers there? Can they pay for what they want to buy? (Ask me sometime to tell you about the time I booked a $2 million order at a company with a $50,000 credit line). By doing a good job here, you eliminate a lot of wasted sales time.

This part of the sales process is a also good diagnostic on future success. Imagine a salesperson who cannot get answers to any of these questions.

How effective will they be in identifying and selling a specific piece of business.

Sales Management Activities

As a sales manager, you need to put together a list of key questions (preferably as part of an account profile) and get your salespeople to use it as part of their survey process. This also allows you to get solid, quick reviews on progress that might include these questions:

Have any new names been added to the list?
Have they identified at least one person to talk to at that organization?
When is the survey call scheduled?
What is the status?

You can see how, as a manager, this makes this part of the process easy to manage. Either the salesperson is adding new names (or they are not); they either know a person (or they do not); and they either have a survey call scheduled (or they do not). Of course they can do all of these things and get no results. If this is the case, you now have to look into the **quality** of the efforts, but the first key question is, "Are the prospecting activities taking place?"

From the sales perspective, Step 1 ends when both you and the salesperson agree on the amount of time they are to spend in trying to sell the customer. In your monthly reviews, you and the salesperson can agree on the following course of action for each customer/prospect on the list:

Invest more time to find out more about the customer/prospect
Move on to the next step
Stop activities for the foreseeable future
Take another look in 6 months (or 3 months or whatever)

The goal is for both you and your salesperson to agree that the first step has been completed.

Step One Summary

A lot of good management boils down to knowing what questions to ask-and when. And listening to what the answers tell you. If your plan calls for new customers, the following are the key questions:

How much time does each salesperson need to spend on finding new customers?

Which prospects seem to meet our definition of "good?" Are there enough of them?

What is our process for learning about customers? What do we need to know about them, upfront?

Are the salespeople doing the things they need to do?

Are they getting the right results or do you need to work with some of them to help them improve their prospecting skills?

Section 6.4 Decision-Making Process (DMP) Identification/Qualification (Step 2)

This is the step where the salesperson tries to identify the Decision-Making Process within the customer. This would make up the second half of what has formerly been called prospecting.

This process has two distinct parts:

The first involves the process, itself. How does an opportunity or a need within a customer move from the person that has it to an order?

The second part involves the people involved in that process. Who is involved in the process?

As a manager, your first job is to help the salespeople understand what they need to do to address these issues. Your second job is to work with them to ensure that the activities take place and that the results are what you want.

The Process

Every organization has some unique-ness and that is one of the things that makes the sales process so difficult. In one company, they may have formal requirements involving requisitions and budget approval processes and in another organization, one person might have the authority to buy almost anything they want with seemingly limitless authority. Successful salespeople try to learn how the process works **before** they invest too much time in working on a particular piece of business.

A good sales manager is going to ask some pointed questions about the customer's Decision-Making Process (DMP) very early in the sales process:

Does this organization use a formal budget?
When does this process start?
How is it approved?
When is it approved?
What criteria do they use to justify expenditures?
Do they use requisitions? Specifications?
How do requisitions/specifications turn into Request For Quotes?
Do they do formal quoting? Informal quoting?
What kind of vendor certification processes exist?

Note that these are all process questions and the goal is to ensure that the salesperson understands the processes within the customer organization. This is critical because the DMP changes from Customer to Customer, from Product to Product and from Time to Time. (If you are paying attention, you might also note that these questions seem to fit right in with the questions we asked the salesperson to find out earlier.

These questions, too, should be part of the account profile.)

These questions have two purposes: the first is that the salesperson needs to know these answers to sell effectively. The other is that if the salesperson is unable to get answers to many of these questions, there is a problem with the approach that coaching or training might solve.

Example

Just for fun, let's take the first question and see what we can do with it: Does this organization have a formal budget?

On the first level, we know that if they have a budget (and it's likely we are not in it,) our first mission will be to understand how they can change a budget during the year.

Think about a salesperson making a call on a new prospect in July that has a fiscal year that starts in January. No matter how interested the person is, what is the reality of selling them something? This is a question the sales manager needs to discuss with the salesperson.

What if the salesperson is unable to get an answer to the question at all? What if the people they are talking with cannot answer the question? What does it tell us about the people the salesperson is calling on? What if the people know but will not answer the question? What are they telling us about the "reality" of doing business with them? And what does it tell the sales manager about the quality of the sales effort?

People

The second half of the equation involves the people. As with process, there are different people involved in the sales process in different types of organizations. In Customer A, Mary Smith with the title of Purchasing Manager may have 100% of the authority to make purchasing decisions on your product. In Customer B, Joe Jones may have the exact same job title but may have almost no authority.

The key is to understand the people involved in the process described above and the role they play.

There are two questions that the salesperson needs to ask that will greatly help to clarify this issue:

Describe your job?
What goals are you focused on this year?

The first is an open-ended question that invites some rambling but if the salesperson listens carefully, they will get some insight into "who" the person is. The second question is much more pointed and gets at reality. Comparing the two answers often tells things that either answer might not.

Remember, too, that there is often a direct correlation between the number of contacts in an organization and both the sales volume and the profit margins.   Have your salespeople identified enough people, in the right places, to be effective?

As a sales manager, you need to work with your salespeople to help them get the answers to these questions.   And if you are not certain that the salesperson is calling on the right people, just ask them these two questions and listen to their answers.

TAC versus PUC, Again

In every organization there is a struggle, often seen and sometimes silent, between the people that want things and the people that buy them or authorize them. For the sake of discussion, we will describe the DMP within organizations as having two distinct halves with a transition point between them.

On the left half of the equation are the Total Acquisition Cost or TAC people.   They have a need. They need the best widget possible to build the part or to repair the part.   They are less concerned about the unit cost than they are about the overall value.

On the right half of the equation are the Per Unit Cost folks or PUCs, pronounced pukes.

These people reduce everything to the lowest common denominator, per unit price.

So if the article costs 1% less and lasts only 80% as long as the product you are selling, they will buy the competitive product.

As early as possible in the sales process, your salespeople need to understand who is the heaviest kid on the seesaw. Will the decision be made by the TAC people or the PUC people?

As an example, if the PUC people will decide what to buy, there is less value in spending time in engineering getting the technical people to like your product. Instead, your salespeople need to work with the PUCs and build good relationships so that you at least have a fighting chance to get it by being the cheapest (yuk!) when it gets there.

The Transition that holds these two parts together in an organization is called "Reqs and Specs." Sometimes these processes are formal and sometimes informal but they occur if at least two people are involved in buying a product or service. The first group of people decide what they want and then they hand it off to someone else who buys it.

You can get great insight into the relative power of each of these groups by understanding how it works within a customer. And there are only about five different approaches:

Generic spec. In the case of a generic spec, the person that wants it writes it up and sends it along to someone that has the authority to buy anything they want from any supplier as long as it meets the general specifications. In this sort organization (or on this sort of product), the PUCs have all the power.

Spec or Equivalent. In this case, the person that wants it specifies a certain type of product/service but acknowledges that it can be an equivalent. This is like the physician that writes a prescription for a certain drug but the pharmacist sells you the generic equivalent. In this case, the PUCs still have almost all the power-assuming that they are the ones that decide the "equivalent" part of the spec.

<u>Spec, only.</u> In this case, the person that wants it tells the PUC to buy a specific product or service from a certain supplier. The TAC has almost all the power.

<u>Spec, Direct.</u> In this case, the person that wants it has the authority to buy it directly from the supplier of choice, bypassing the formal purchasing function. Maintenance people with credit cards and $500 worth of authority are one example and VPs of Manufacturing with an approved budget and a stack of Purchase Orders is another example. In this case, the PUCs are irrelevant-except that you need to keep in their good graces for future opportunities.

As a manager, you have to quiz the salespeople on their understanding of this process, who is involved-and of critical importance-who has the power?

Think about the role that each of these might play for your kind of sale:

Engineering
Executive Management
Environmental
Maintenance
Operations
Outsourcing

Purchasing
QA

Which of these areas are important? Does the salesperson have the appropriate contacts in each area?

Section Summary

Successful selling requires a clear understanding of the customer's processes for purchasing what you sell and the people involved. Before you invest a lot of sales resource in working with a prospect (or on a new opportunity in an existing customer), work with the salespeople to check their understanding of the following:

What process do they use to buy what you are selling?
Who is involved?
How does the requisition/specification process work?
What half of the equation (TAC vs PUC) has the power in this transaction?

Section 6.5 Opportunity Identification/Qualification (Step 3)

The next step in the sales process is to find a "real" opportunity. This means finding a piece of business that is important enough for both the salesperson and the customer to work on. (We are describing a sales situation—not a situation where the customer is simply reordering something they have always bought from you).

This is one of the hardest parts of selling (and most sales failures occur here). For many salespeople the logic goes like this:

I sell it; they buy it; they are talking to me—therefore there must be an opportunity.

As we all know, nothing could be further from the truth. People talk to salespeople for many reasons, including the fact that they are bored. How many sales presentations have you listened to over the years with no intention of buying, simply to be polite? Much worse than that, however, is that many organizations are required to get multiple bids on items they purchase. They are not required to take the low bidder in most instances but they have to get multiple quotes. How many times is your salesperson simply working hard to get an opportunity to be the third quote?

This step of the sale really has two different parts:

Finding a potential piece of business
Determining its reality

Finding a potential piece of business...

As with the other two parts of the process, sales management can provide real value by helping the salesperson to construct <u>activities</u> that aid in finding opportunities. Think about what those activities might be for your business:

A facility tour

A capabilities presentation to senior management of the customer

Meeting with engineers to identify products in design or re-design

A review of quality problems with the current supplier

A review of delivery problems with the current supplier

Lack of customer purchases due to an outdated technology

High repair costs due to the failure of a supplied part

Lack of sales due to the high cost of supplied parts

Over-specified parts (Too much value for the application)

What are the activities that your salespeople need to do, on a regular basis to find "real" opportunities? Where should they be doing them? With TAC people? With PUC people? How often?

The key to this part of the process is to have a clear "Value Proposition" in place. The value proposition answers the question of why the customer should care. Too often, salespeople make a fatal error—they tell the customer what they are offering without ever addressing the most important point—why they should switch from their current supplier.

Often, salespeople assume that they know the reason—Per Unit Cost. If, for example, their product is cheaper, they will get the business, right? Sometimes, sometimes not. Depends on whether you are calling on TACs or PUCs and just how important that particular issue is to the organization.

Remember that in a sales situation (where we are selling against an existing supplier), we must find one of two things:

A problem that they cannot solve (That they care enough about to want to solve) or
An opportunity that they cannot exploit (And they see the value in exploiting it).

Most salespeople are pretty good about looking for the parts of the above statement that are not included in the parentheses. The second part is more difficult and many salespeople brush past it without really considering it. As an example, one salesperson found that they could save the customer about 3% on one of the components of their finished product. The only problem was that the component, itself, was only about 1% of the total cost of the product. On the priority list, that part just didn't come up. Yet the salesperson worked diligently on it for about two years before finally giving up.

Determining its Reality

The second half of the process is to determine the reality of a particular piece of business. We may have the solution, we may have the price, we may meet all the requirements—and still not get the business. Sometimes this is due to the old "brother-in-law as competitor" or even to under the table payoffs—but mostly, it's just a lack of interest.

So your salesperson comes back from a call and describes the brilliant presentation just made to a customer. You feel pretty good about the customer and the person (people) they are speaking with seem to be the right people.

Now comes the best part: Are we really in contention? Is there any real reason why we think that they are seriously considering us for the upcoming order?

We have developed a list of "diagnostic" questions. We call them diagnostic because if your salesperson will ask them early in the process—and of the right people, they will get some very powerful insight into the "reality" of the opportunity.

These questions test three things:

Are we working in a qualified organization?
Are we talking to the right person (people)?
Is this a real piece of business (for us)?

We recommend that the salesperson ask the following questions: Diagnostic Questions

1. Is it budgeted?
2. What is the application?
3. What is the exact quantity required?
4. Who is the competition?
5. What is the target price?
6. When does the order have to be placed?

7. Why would you buy it from a different vendor (this time)?

Is it budgeted? This is a very innocuous question and most salespeople ask it. If the customer cannot (or will not) answer it, you might have a problem. Most organizations have some sort of budget and if the purchase is budgeted and they have not ever spoken with us, you can bet that they got some other supplier's numbers so we know we have some competition.

What is the application? This is another straightforward question that should be readily answered. The salesperson asks this question to find out if the person they are speaking with really understands what they are buying and also to ensure that the specifications match the application and that there is an "apples for apples" comparison. What does it tell you if the customer cannot (or will not) answer the question?

What is the exact quantity required? Beware of answers that sound like this: "5, 50 or 500." Remember that if it is budgeted, they had to put a quantity in there. What is it? And if the person does not know how many are really needed...

Who is the competition? This is another simple question that is needed for apples to apples comparison (and maybe pricing strategies.) And if the customer will not tell the salesperson who the competition is...

What is the target price? This question begins to separate out the best salespeople from the good ones. The best always ask this question. The information is needed to check with the answers on application, budget and competition. But the real value is in finding out if the customer really wants to do business with you. If they will not give you a target price range, do they really want to do business with you? And if they do not know it (and it's budgeted)????? There is nothing unethical about asking this question and how many organizations have a real need for something and no idea about what they want to pay for it?

When does the order have to be placed? A great way to separate the unreal from the real is to get the customer to define the timeframe of need. A lot of times a customer will ask for information or a sample and when you ask them when you should follow up they give you a vague answer such as "Oh, in a month or two…" How real is that business?

Why would you buy it from a different vendor (this time)? Of all of the great sales questions, this one may be the best. By asking it, the salesperson tries to define a reason why the customer might make a different buying decision. Remember that the salesperson is supposed to have a good Value Proposition going in, but if the customer cannot articulate a reason to change, they probably will not (or perhaps, the salesperson is not talking with the right person.) Either way, this question gets to the heart of the matter.

Note that this is not the same as asking, "What do I have to do to get this order?" That question is assumed to mean that the only thing standing between the salesperson and the order is Unit Price. Wrong question at this stage. Instead, the salesperson should ask an open-ended question and listen carefully to the answer.

Having laid these questions out, there might be one or two more questions that you could add and maybe even one or two you want to delete although I would recommend keeping the ones above. Remember that the purpose of these questions is to test the validity of the opportunity. Failure to get answers (or coherent answers) does not mean that the salesperson should abandon the opportunity but that they now know that a problem exists and they might want to do something about it. (We studied over 10,000 sales opportunities and determined that if the salesperson is unable to get answers to at least 4 of the questions above, their chances of booking the order are less than 1%).

Ideally, your salesperson will ask these questions of multiple contacts on major opportunities and compare answers

As a sales manager, you should ask your salespeople these same questions on major opportunities to get an understanding of how real the opportunity is, follow-up actions to get to the truth and how much time they should spend working a given opportunity.

One other key point to investigate on an opportunity involves the customer's effort. If all of the activity rests with our organization, how interested is the customer, really?

Remember that any time spent on an "unreal" opportunity is time that cannot be spent working on an opportunity that can be booked.

Summary

Work with your salesperson to define the activities needed to find real pieces of business. Make certain that they are doing them at the right organizations with the right people. Make sure that they are doing enough of them.

Help your salespeople to understand the reality of each opportunity by having formal processes in place that allow you to quickly diagnose problems—early in the sales process.

What kind of opportunities are your salespeople supposed to find?

What activities is your salesperson supposed to do to find opportunities?
Are they doing them?
Enough of them?
Well enough?

What activities is your salesperson supposed to do to determine the "reality" of each opportunity?
Are they doing them?
Enough of them?
Well enough?

Section 6.6 Qualification by the Prospect/Customer (Step 4)

Assuming that you have a real customer; are dealing with the decision-maker; and have found a real opportunity, the next step in the sale is to present a solution and get the customer to agree that it will work for them. Sounds simple enough and often it is, but sometimes, it isn't.

Asking your organization to work on something does not mean that you are qualified.

A call from a major company that is not a customer now may not mean anything at all. If you are not approved for that product at that company, you cannot get the order.

Many salespeople put this step before Step 3. The assumption is that if we show the customer something really neat, it will create an opportunity. In fact, there are thousands of times when we go through the qualification process, are approved but still do not get orders. And this also explains why some customers are loath to go through the qualification process, at all. For example, how many times have your salespeople run into the following situation?

They find a potential new customer and make a presentation. They are told that there are already five approved vendors for that product or service and that they do not need any more.

This is not a failure of the qualification process but a failure in the opportunity identification process. The salesperson has not given the customer a good enough reason to go through the steps required to get qualified.

Sometimes, it seems to work when a salesperson tries to do the qualification first—but this is the exception, not the rule. And how many times have you seen a salesperson do a demonstration or present qualification information—only to have to it again when there is a real piece of business?

As a manager, your efforts should be to focus on both parts of this step:

Does what we are proposing address the customer's concerns?
Does the salesperson understand how the customer will answer this question?

Our proposed solution

The first thing to pay attention to is: Does what we are proposing address the customer's concerns? Or, having identified a need, does our solution really address it? Many times, we try to fit our solution in where it does not really belong. This not only rarely results in a sale but often makes it harder for the

131

salesperson to go back and explore future opportunities.

So on key opportunities, get the salesperson to run through the need/opportunity and our proposed solution and see if they match up.

The customer's evaluation process

In Step 2, the salesperson was supposed to identify the decision-making process for the product/service they are trying to sell. Part of this involves the process the customer uses for evaluating/approving alternatives and the people involved. I cannot overstress the importance of this question. Take as an example, a salesperson that wants a customer to switch from purchasing Widget A to Widget B. We assume that form, fit and function are the same, but unless the right people in the customer's organization agree with this assessment, there is no way that we can ever sell the product.

Let's construct a list of the <u>activities</u> that salespeople can do which are part of the qualification process:

Providing literature
Product/service demonstrations
Providing samples
Developing specifications
Providing references

Others?

What are the activities that your salespeople must do to help the customer decide if our product/service meets their needs?

The second half of the question is: What are the customer activities that are required to determine if your product or service meets their needs?

Reviewing literature/specifications
Testing samples
Checking references

Others?

And, who is involved in these processes?

Is it one person? Or a committee? Do they all have the same criteria? Or different?

Do not let your salespeople be fooled by the simple answer. A purchasing person might solicit information and they might place the order, but who else has to decide if your product will work? Is it someone in marketing? Sales? Operations? Manufacturing? Engineering? Quality? Safety?

To put it very simply, before a customer can buy something they have never bought before (from you), they have to agree that it will work. This also explains why we quote a lot and don't get a lot of orders.

Allowing us to quote does not mean that we are qualified.

Qualification essentials

Generally, the customer evaluates three things. Two of these are often formal process and one is almost never formal, but it is always there. The three main qualification ingredients are:

The product/service
The company
The salesperson

The product/service

Most salespeople understand this one. In fact, this is the one they know best. Customers talk about this one the most, as well. How does it work? When can we get it? What are its features? What are its competitive advantages?

These are all questions that help the customer to decide if they **can** use it. (Note that the fact they can use it does not mean they will but this decision is definitely a prerequisite for a sale.)

For the most part, the customer looks at issues similar to these:

Form, fit and function: (Especially if you are attempting to dislodge an existing application). This means—does it meet what is currently being used?

Quality: This is a subjective term and you need to understand what the customer means.

> Does this refer to a measurement of inbound inspection, field failure, rework, or scrap? Or is it really another way of describing how well the product performs?

Stocking levels: Or how quickly can I get it?

What other things might the customer consider important in evaluating your product or service?

The job of the salesperson is to understand how each is being evaluated and the "weight" accorded to each. For instance, are they willing to trade lesser availability for better quality?

Ask the salesperson how the customer will evaluate what we are selling and who is involved. Is it a formal process? Do they know how it works? Do they know the results the customer is looking for? Do they know how long it takes? If not, these are good questions to get them to ask.

If you are in distribution, part of this question also involves the additional ring of services provided by the manufacturer's reps or the manufacturer such as extended warranties, technical support and on-going innovation.

The company

Over the past several years, this has become a much more important part of the equation. Formal vendor evaluation, certification and ranking is becoming more and more prevalent. Some organizations insist that you be on an Approved Vendor List before you can even make sales calls. (And some organizations that have AVLs disregard them all the time, by the way.)

One of the simplest questions to check with your salesperson is this one: Is our company approved to do business with this customer (for this item)? Remember that you can be approved for some items, but not all. If the salesperson is unsure (or if they are unsure how to get approved), you can help them.

The customer often cares about (and rates) these issues:

Financial stability
Technical approaches/ideas
Capabilities
Ease of working with an organization
Responsiveness

What other things does the customer consider about your organization?

The salesperson

Few customers have formal salespeople evaluations although some do. Those that do tend to focus on the following criteria:

Follow-through skills
Product knowledge
Integrity
Problem-solving abilities
Credibility
Willingness to go to bat for customer's interests
Presentation skills
Knowledge of competitor's products
Industry knowledge
Appropriate frequency of sales calls

Using this list, how would you rate your salespeople? Are they good at these issues? Who specifically needs improvement in what areas? (You might keep this in mind for our later discussion on development issues.)

Most of the time, however, this is an informal evaluation with a lot of emphasis on personality. Keep this in mind when you are hiring, however, so that you build a successful profile personality for your customer base and hire to those standards.

Objections

Joseph C. Ellers

This is also the part of the sales process where objections tend to occur. As a manager, you need to pay attention to the objections that the salesperson is getting. IS there a pattern there?

For example, if the prospective customer routinely tells us that our price is too high, is this true? Or perhaps are we not presenting our story to the right people for evaluation? Or are we are talking to the right people, but doing the right things?

Sales management should track the kinds of objections that are received and where they come from within the prospect/customer organization. The purpose is to determine whether the marketing strategy needs to be changed or the salesperson needs to be educated.

Summary

Pay attention to the following issues:

Does what we are proposing address the customer's concerns?
Does the salesperson understand how the customer will answer this question?

What are the activities that your salespeople must do to help the customer decide if our product/service meets their needs?

What are the customer activities that are required to determine if your product or service meets their needs? Who is involved in these processes?

How do they evaluate:

Our product/service?
Our company?
The salesperson?

What is the pattern of objections? In the territory? At specific customers?

Section 6.7 Quoting/Proposals (Step 5)

The fifth step in the sales process is where the product or service is officially offered and where a lot of the negotiating comes in. This is a critical part of the sales process and one that should be managed very aggressively because this where all sales come from and where most margin is lost.

From a management perspective, there is also the need to work with the salespeople to fully understand the exactly what the customer needs at this stage of the sales process.

There are three key recognitions here:

Is the opportunity really at the quote/proposal stage?
What kind of activities are required?

Are the quotes reflective of our strategy?

Are we there yet?

The first question is, Are we there yet? Many salespeople are in a hurry to get to the quote stage. Many salespeople actually begin the sales process by asking for an opportunity to quote. (I guess the goal is to show how cheap we can be up front, thereby eliminating any opportunity to add value later.)

And some prospects/customers greet salespeople with opportunities to quote.

The problem is that there are several different kinds of quotes and the salesperson needs to understand what kind of quoting situation they are involved in. There are four different types of quotes:

Buy
Budget
Ballpark
Blow-off

Buy

A quote for buy is the kind we want. This means that the following statements are true:

We are dealing with a qualified customer
We are dealing with the decision-maker
We have a real opportunity
The customer agrees that our proposed solution will work

(Note that these statements are the test for whether we have completed each of the previous steps of the sales process.)

All of these can be true and we will still not get the order, but if we quote and any of these is not true, the odds against us getting the order are astronomical.

Budget

A lot of quotes are really budgetary. Someone wants something and they do not know how much it costs so they use you to find out. This does not mean that they intend to buy it from you just that they might want it. A budgetary quote cannot be a real quote because it has not been budgeted. Remember the first question we ask in trying the clarify the reality of an opportunity is, Is this budgeted?

Some quotes are obviously budgetary. For example, the customer's fiscal year is ending and they are asking your organization to quote on a major purchase which takes at least 45-60 days to get. You know that they could not possibly issue a purchase order before their year ends so you have to suspect that the request is budgetary.

The only real warning here is that if the salesperson asks "Budget or buy?," the answer is almost always "Buy," even if it isn't. The way to check is to see if the salesperson can clearly define that the first four steps have been completed—to the satisfaction of the customer.

Ballpark

A ballpark quote is a quote that can occur anywhere in the sales process. The purpose of a ballpark quote is to see if your are "in the ballpark" on pricing. There may not even be a pending purchase here so getting an order is unlikely. This is an indication of interest—maybe—or it may simply be that the customer needs another quote to beat up their existing supplier.

The way to investigate this is to ask the salesperson what the value proposition is. Find out if there is a reason why the customer might change. If that reason has been identified—and the customer agrees that it is a valid reason, it might be a valid <u>ballpark </u>quote. Otherwise, the quote really falls into the final category…

Blow-off

Blow-off quotes come from a variety of reasons. Some are simply to get rid of salespeople. If they send the salesperson away with something to quote, they leave easier. Some are simply the "third" quote where a customer is required to get three quotes (not to take the lowest quote, mind you), so your organization provides the third quote.

Some quotes are used to beat up the existing supplier. In many cases, quotes are solicited from people that are not on the Approved Vendor List for this purpose.

Whatever the reason, a large percentage of the quotes your organization has outstanding at any given time are probably blow-off quotes. As a sales manager, you need to ask enough questions about the opportunity to understand if this is happening (often.)

What kind of activities are required: quotes or proposals?

Many times when this point is reached, the salesperson assumes that the customer merely wants to confirm the pricing and availability. For this reason, a lot of salespeople spend little time thinking about what the real question might be so they view a quote as a confirming document.

There are times, however, when the quote needs to be a selling document. In this case, the tool used should be a proposal and not a quote. For our definitions, a quote covers price/delivery/warranty issues while a proposal is a more comprehensive document that addresses questions about some of the more subtle aspects of the product/service along with information about the organization (and maybe even the salesperson.) Remember that these three things are the areas evaluated by the customer when making a purchasing decision.

Listed below are some of the areas where the salesperson should issue more than just a confirming document:

New customer. If you have never done business with a particular organization before, there will be a lot of uncertainty. By putting a more substantial proposal in their hands, you make it easier for them to make a different buying decision.

New individual. Same as above. Even though the customer may be the same if you have a new person, they might need some additional justification for making a purchasing decision.

New product/service. Same as both above. Even though the individual may have bought other things from your organization, when you ask them to do something different, you need to do something different as well.

Committee decision. In this case, you know that a committee will review data and make a final decision. To increase your chances of success, you need to put a lot of information in the hands of the committee—hoping that your competition only gives them a price.

Higher price. Whenever you know that you are not the cheapest you probably need to remind the customer of the reasons why they should pay more.

How many of your current opportunities might "need" proposals?

What are the elements that you might include in a "Proposal" as opposed to a "Quote?"

Are the quotes reflective of your strategy?

You can tell a lot about where your business headed by looking at what is being quoted or proposed. Almost all of your orders will come from your quote backlog so an important consideration is, "Does my quote backlog reflect my strategy?"

In the first section, we talked about the kind of business that you want for your organization. It addressed three key areas:

What do you want to sell?
Who do you want to sell it to?
What does a good order look like?

If you answered these questions, a quick look at your quote backlog can tell you who is doing a good job of responding and who is not—and where they are having difficulty.

For example, if you really wean to increase sales in a certain product or service, it's a fair bet that you should be growing the quote backlog. Are you?

The same would be true for a target market or customer segment. If you want more sales to come from a certain group of customers, we have to be quoting those customers. And it also holds for orders. Are your salespeople quoting the right kinds of orders? Are they beginning to look more like what you want?

This is the easiest part of the sales process to monitor **and** you can still have an impact on the outcome. It's easy to monitor the sales but there is little to be done at that point but at the quote stage, you can actually help the salesperson to develop the closing strategy or accompany them on calls for key pieces of business.

So if you want to start a more proactive sales management effort, this is a great place to start it.

Summary

Begin by helping your salespeople to understand whether they are actually in the quote stage or not. Make certain that you use either quotes or proposals, as appropriate, depending on the sales situation. Manage the sales process better by paying attention to the quote backlog.

Is the opportunity really at the quote/proposal stage? Is this a quote for buy, budget, ballpark or blowoff?

What kind of activities are required? Does this opportunity warrant a quote or proposal? What should be in the proposal?

Are the quotes reflective of our strategy? Are your salespeople quoting the right kinds of orders? Are they beginning to look more like what you want?

Section 6.8 Closing the sale (Step 6)

The final step of the sales process is the close. Many sales training programs focus heavily on the closing process. For most people in the business-to-business sales arena, those tactics are worthless. In the first place, we generally do not have the luxury of forcing closes because that creates a bad atmosphere with people that we need to work with on an on-going basis. Secondly, many of them do not work.

As a sales manager, you have the following closing considerations:

Are the closing attempts occurring at the right time?
Are the closing attempts done correctly?
Are you managing the process?

Might have been the right place, but it must have been the wrong time

There are two specific types of closes—real closes where the salesperson wants to get an order and trial closes where the salesperson wants to get commitment to move toward a close.

Trial closes can (and should) be used throughout the sales process as a way of building commitment. Trial closes are great ways to determine if the salesperson has completed a specific sales step. As an example, the seven questions presented in Step 3 (Opportunities), are in fact all trial closes because a willingness to answer them signifies a level of commitment.

Real closes, on the other hand, can only occur at the end of the process—after the other five steps have been completed. For example, if the quote was for Budget, Ballpark or Blow-off, a real close is inappropriate because we have not given a real quote. The same would be true if we were not certain that our solution had been approved; if we suspected that there was no real reason to switch; if we do not think we are dealing with the right person or if we do not think the organization can really afford what we are selling—for example.

Unfortunately, for many salespeople and customers alike, the close is a very difficult time—charged with emotion and potential conflict. The main reason for this is that the close is not done with the right preparation and at the right time. The problem is almost always a matter of incorrect timing. If the question is asked and the customer does not see it coming (because the bases have not been touched), it creates conflict and actually diminishes the chance of getting the order—even if the customer had intended to give it to the salesperson all along.

If the sales process has been done correctly, the close is a natural, logical extension of all that has gone before—not a separate action. Work with your salespeople to make the close better by doing it at the right time.

Are the closing attempts done correctly?

Probably the most impact that sales management can have on the close is to ensure that the close, itself, is done correctly. There are several key factors here:

Scheduled
Closing question
The wisdom of Sampson

Scheduled. For all major pieces of business, there should be a close scheduled with the customer. There is some very significant psychology that surrounds a scheduled close. If the customer commits to a time when they are going to give the salesperson a yes/no answer, several advantages accrue to the salesperson. Most importantly, that commitment pushes the customer in the direction of giving the salesperson an ultimate "yes."

Further, it takes all of the curse off of the close, itself, because the customer has given permission for the close to occur.

Closing question. At various times, you need to set up a closing situation and roleplay it with your salespeople. They will hate it (you might, too), but you need to listen to the way in which they attempt to close business. A key to closing is that the salesperson must ask a question—not make a statement—that requires a yes/no answer. For example, "May I have the PO number?" Too often, salespeople do not ask closing questions but instead make closing statements such as, "We'd like to help you out with that widget."

This is not a question and no action is required from the customer. It accomplishes one goal—its lets the customer know that an order would be appreciated without appearing pushy. But it does not really accomplish the goal of being a "real" closing call.

The wisdom of Sampson. "Sampson" is not a misprint. I did not mean Solomon. There is an old saying that Sampson slew 1000 Philistines with the jawbone of an ass…and that every day as many sales are killed in the same way. The wisdom of Sampson is that once the closing question is asked, your salesperson needs to shut up. Often salespeople will ask a good closing question and then begin to answer it before allowing the customer to do so.

The silence after a closing question is asked is very powerful and a professional salesperson is not afraid of that silence and uses it to their advantage.

Managing the Process

There is value in managing the close portion of the sales process. Some of the things to pay attention to are:

Scheduled closing calls
Effectiveness, by category

Margins

Scheduled closing calls. One measure of sales effectiveness is to pay attention to the scheduled closing calls, by salesperson. If a salesperson begins to have a decline in the number of scheduled closing calls, there may be a problem. Pay attention.

Effectiveness. For some strange reason, many sales organizations do not track the close ratio. At a minimum, it should be tracked at the organization level. What percentage of quotes do we close? What percentage of the dollar value do we close? If you can get a handle on these, you can do a better job of forecasting business and also see trends (up or down) with some time left to influence them before they become acute. Many sales organizations also pay attention to close ratio, by salesperson, by product, and by customer. These are excellent diagnostics as they alert the manager to specific problems. What if one salesperson has a higher close rate than everyone else? What is different? Is it a good problem (better opportunities) or a bad problem (not working enough opportunities)? What if we have a significantly lower close ratio on a certain group of products? What if we have a lower close ratio on certain customers? Certain groups of customers? All of these can help the sales manager to focus on the real problems in their organization.

Margins. Price and margin erosion is easily diagnosed at the quote stage. For the outstanding quotes, what is happening to the margins? At key customers? For key products? On strategic

151

opportunities? By paying attention to this part of the process, the sales manager can get insight into market conditions.

Summary

Effective sales management focuses on two specific areas: helping salespeople to close at the right time with the right closing tools. Further, a professional sales manager does not try to "manage" booked business but uses the information to try and improve what will happen on future closing opportunities.

Are the closing attempts occurring at the right time?

Are the closing attempts done correctly? Is the close scheduled? Is a closing question asked?

Are you managing the process? Pay attention to the following:

Scheduled closing calls
Effectiveness, by category
Margins

Sales Management Self-Audit

Rate each answer on a scale of 1-12 with 1 being "Not at all" and 12 being "Totally."

_____Our organization has a clearly defined, sequential sales process.

_____We know which part of the process we want to focus on: TAC vs PUC

(Trigger, Design, Purchasing, Order)

_____We have management systems that reinforce the message of where the want sales time to be focused.

_____Our organizational resources are aligned with our sales strategy. (As an example, if we are trying to win business at the Order stage, we have everything the customer might need in stock (or we can get it), all the time.

_____We manage activities at each phase of the sales process.

_____We track opportunities at each phase of the sales process.

_____Sales management has the ability to intervene in sales activities—not to just get reports on what has happened.

_____We have defined the steps of the sales process that are done best/worst by our salespeople and we have on-going activities to improve our worst areas.

Add your numbers and give yourself a score: _____. (Add back the 4 points I took away from you in the scoring process—just for reading this Section.)

Section 7.0 The Perfect Sales Call

The sales call is the building block of the sales process. Almost all of the value added by the salesperson (remember the three evaluations of product/service, company and salesperson) comes during the qualification stage of the sales process. The customer's question is simple: does this particular salesperson add enough value for me to commit my time? There are all kinds of ways in which a salesperson can add value but the most important in today's world (and I would hypothesize that this has always been the case), is to help the customer to solve a problem or exploit an opportunity.

The customer may not realize that a problem exists and in this case it is the responsibility of the salesperson to help them see it. Over the years, however, the value proposition for customers has been presented to salespeople in a lot of different ways.

When we ask salespeople why a customer should see them, we get a variety of answers:

Because they like us. Almost since the beginning of time, it has been assumed that this was important. It's why we entertain. It's why we ask about their hobbies. It's why we have historically hired the personable people for sales jobs. There is nothing wrong with being liked but it's not the best reason to ask a customer to do business with us. It's been said that people do business with a company because they have to or because they want to. That's probably true but there are a lot of reasons why a customer might "want" to do business with us that have nothing to do with "liking" our salespeople.

Because we have something new. One of the great laments of some salespeople is that their company is just not giving them anything new to talk about. The underlying assumption there is that everyone at every customer already knows everything about everything we are offering to sell. That's almost never true. It's also almost never true that simply having something new creates an opportunity. How would you feel if a door-to-door peddler came by your house every evening at dinner time and showed you something new? Or if your insurance agent called you every time they got a new kind of policy to sell. "Hey, we just added boat insurance and I sure would like to tell you about it." One small problem, you don't own a boat and have no intention of getting one—but your insurance agent has "something new."

Guess what? Every day a lot of salespeople call their boatless customers to tell them about boat insurance.

And taking this analogy one step further, let's say you have a boat and that it is insured. The fact that the insurance people have a new policy might not mean anything unless you have decided that you need a new policy.

Joseph C. Ellers

Newness, in and of itself, is never a good reason to ask for an appointment. There needs to be an understanding of both need and interest.

<u>Because we have something better.</u> This discussion sounds a lot like the one above. Your company has developed a better mousetrap. Your salespeople decide to tell all of their customers about it. Again, what if they have no need or interest?

You can do a great diagnostic with your salespeople by asking this simple question:
What's in it for the customer?

Before your salesperson tries to schedule a call, get them to tell you why the customer should even talk to them. Get them to give you the reason why this particular person might have a particular need now that might make them want to give the salesperson an appointment.

Section 7.1 Overview

At this point, you probably want to see how a few of your salespeople try to set appointments. You also need to use a few simple tools to see if you have a problem. One of the simplest ways to analyze the effectiveness of a salesperson is to look at the problems a salesperson encounters as they try to set sales appointments. There are several specific results (or non-results) that you are looking for:

No need of scheduled calls. This one has been gaining a lot of ground recently—especially as an excuse. Our observation has shown that most of the effective salespeople have scheduled calls. Or to put it another way, they are expected at 10:00 on Tuesday—not early in the week or even sometime Tuesday morning—but at a specific time. As companies have rationalized, down-sized, right-sized or whatever, there are truly fewer people to see—and their time is at a premium. The end result is that they just don't have as much time as they used to—especially to see salespeople who do not add value. Some salespeople are using this excuse to not schedule appointments but to schedule "drop bys" instead. "They don't give appointments, they just want me to 'drop by' and if they have anything to talk with me about, they'll see me," is one I hear a lot.

People that have a real need will give you an appointment (no matter how busy they are) so this is one way of checking the reality of an opportunity. If you review your salesperson's calendar and they do not have several appointments scheduled, it's a good indication that you have a problem.

Inability to schedule calls. Some salespeople do not have scheduled calls because they do not think they are supposed to have them. Other salespeople do not have scheduled calls because they cannot get them. When you want to see someone at a customer location (and you ask the salesperson to set it up), how does it go? Can they get the appointment?

Do some of your salespeople seem to have no problem calling on lower levels of the organization, but complain about an inability to see other people they need to see? If they cannot schedule calls, there might be a problem with technique. One of the worst ways to try to set an appointment sounds like this, "I'm Joe Ellers with ABC Company. I'll be in your area next Tuesday and I would like to drop by and tell you about our company." This is a technique that I hear a lot and it's terrible because it adds no value to the customer. (Unless you assume that there is a huge stack of requisitions for your product setting on the customer's desk because you are the only person in the world they can get it from.)

<u>Customer-Blown appointments</u>. You are making calls with a salesperson and a customer does not show up for an appointment. "He's sorry," the receptionist tells you, "Mr. Jones had an emergency meeting come up." This will happen occasionally but if it is a routine occurrence, you are hearing loudly and clearly from the customer base that the salesperson does a lousy job of establishing the value of the appointment.

<u>Lobby calls.</u> Another sign of poor sales call ability is the lobby call. You've had it happen occasionally so maybe you don't notice, but these are another indication of a problem. Here's how it goes: Your salesperson shows up for a 9:00 appointment and Ms. Smith comes out to the lobby and without even sitting down invites the salesperson to tell her about the call. In this case, the customer is politely telling us that they

are not sure why the call the being made—or worse—they know why and there is little or no value to the call. We might feel good about seeing the customer but what we have really done here is to waste the customer's time. This builds a little wall between the us and the customer. This wall is something that we will have to climb over (if we can) before we get the next appointment.

<u>Long waits.</u>   The final indication that your salesperson has a problem with the customer is the long wait. Again, you've seen this before, you and the salesperson arrive in the lobby at 8:50 for your 9:00 appointment.   You are announced by the receptionist and you wait. 9:00 comes and goes. As does 9:15. At 9:30 or so, you are waved back in to see the customer. They may even give the salesperson some excuse about a phone call or an impromptu meeting. The message is the same. The salesperson adds no value to that customer.

All of these things will happen over the course of a professional lifetime. But if these are frequent events, they are telling you (as a manager) that the salesperson has a problem in the most basic part of the sales process.

This may explain why the salesperson is failing to make quota. It might not be that they do not do good presentations or that their closing skills are not up to snuff but simply that they do not do a good job of setting appointments.

Over the years, we have observed some of the best salespeople in the world and they follow a process. Just like the sale, itself, there are certain things that need to be done, every time, in order, for the sales call to achieve maximum effectiveness. How much of this can be applied to your sales situation?

<u>Summary</u>

As a sales manager, you have to do regular activities:

To help your salespeople to construct good sales calls
To identify problems in your sales force

When working with salespeople, consider the following:

What is their current approach for trying to get sales appointments?

Are their signs that there is a problem:

  No "need" for scheduled calls?
  Inability to schedule calls?
  Customer-blown appointments?
  Lobby calls?
  Long waits?

Section 7.2 Call Preparation

Most athletic contests and wars are won (or lost) in preparation. In the workworld, however, we often fail to prepare. How many times does a salesperson pick up the phone to call a prospect with only a vague notion of what they want to accomplish? And how many call plans are made up between the time the car is parked and the salesperson reaches the lobby?

The Purpose

The first part of the sales call preparation process is to help the salesperson to understand that if they have a clear purpose for each call, they are more likely to be successful. When you ask a lot of salespeople why they are making a specific call, they have vague answers such as "To try to sell them something." This is not nearly clear enough so to help them, ask a couple of important questions:

What do I want this call to accomplish? Before even asking for an appointment, every salesperson should ask this question of themselves. (This is a great tool for sales managers as well.)

There is a long list to pick from:

Find out more about the company
Identify the decision-makers/influencers within the account
Find out more about the people involved in the Decision Making Process
Find out more about how decisions are made
Make a presentation about our company/ product/ capabilities
Identify opportunities
Provide qualification information
Get permission to provide a quote/proposal
Present a quote/proposal
Schedule a closing call
Close a sale

This list is not complete but the salesperson should be very clear about what they want to accomplish on the call. As a sales manager, you might also pay attention to the number of actual sales activities planned for a call. Issues such as resolving backorders or problems with invoices are important—and they lay a foundation for future sales—but they are not **sales** activities.

The second question (which we have covered in some detail earlier) is:

What's in it for the customer? We are trying to get the salesperson to think about the reasons why the customer should give us some of their time. Does the salesperson have a good answer to this question? If they do not, there will be some problems even getting the appointment.

Account Knowledge

With a clear purpose in mind, the next step is to review what we know about a prospect or customer. We will talk in more detail about account profiles and specifically how to use them but all professional sales calls are preceded by a review of what we know about the customer. The reason for this is simple: there is a direct correlation between how much the salesperson knows about a customer and their ability to sell them.

Professional salespeople keep a pretty complete book on their customers and prospects. They know a lot about the organization, what it is trying to accomplish, the main problems it's facing and a lot about the people.

If the proposed call is on a prospect, we expect our account knowledge to be limited. This drives one of our call objectives—to find out more about the prospect on this sales call. A good account profile serves as a prompt that gives salespeople a push toward what they need to know to sell the account.

Many times salespeople lose business at an account because things change and they do not notice. Over the years, we have seen that every change in an account is either an opportunity or a problem— depending on who has the business. If for example, someone is promoted, that might be good news or bad news depending on your relationships—and how that account does business.

Professional salespeople pay attention to changes (and document them). Which customer goals are different from last year? Last quarter? What new processes are they using (that might affect my business?) Which departments are being reorganized? Which people are doing different jobs?

All of these will affect the salesperson's ability to find, get and keep business. How many new opportunities are now available because of changes in the customer base? How much of the salesperson's current business is at risk?

Schedule a "real" sales call (and get agreement on the purpose)

After the salesperson is clear on their goals and on what they know about an account, the next step is to try and schedule an appointment. (I can already hear you telling me that I don't understand and that people just don't give appointments in your business. Key people do give appointments if the salesperson adds value. And remember, part of what we are doing here is also a diagnostic. The simple act of asking for an appointment gives the salesperson insight into the perceived value they offer.)

"Real" Sales Call Defined: Since you may never have given your salespeople a definition of a sales call, let's start with this one:

A sales call is a scheduled appointment (in person or phone) that has the following elements:

A definite day: When setting up a call, "Monday" is a better call than "early next week."

A definite time: "10:00 am" is better than "Monday morning."

A definite person: "Mary Smith" is better than "the purchasing department"

A definite purpose (agreed to in advance by the customer): "Meeting to discuss whether they will consider using our new product in place of the Acme product for the new widget application" is better than "telling them about our new product"

Agreed to in advance by the customer is the key. Large numbers of sales calls fail the last part of the definition. They are vague and often the customer is not really aware of our reason for coming. Many times this is because the salesperson feels that if they tell the customer the exact reason for the visit, the customer will say, "No." But this is really the key. If the customer knows why the salesperson is coming and agrees to it, there is a good chance that an opportunity can be found. If the customer is not sure why you are coming, there is no <u>customer</u> preparation and therefore, a decreased chance of success.

This point cannot be overemphasized because it is one of the key failings of a lot of salespeople. Before your salespeople try to set an appointment, work with them to create a clear sets of questions/statements that define what they want out of the call—then listen to them as they try to set appointments. And remember the fact that your company has a new widget or the fact that your salesperson is going to be in the area next Tuesday is not really a good reason to try and schedule a call.

Written Call Plans

Salespeople that use written call plans are more successful than those who do not. We observed this "phenomena" over a ten year period and found that salespeople with written call plans tend to accomplish over twice as many of their call objectives (76% versus 29%) as salespeople that have "mental" call plans. Further, salespeople that use written call plans tend to make about 160% more than other salespeople.

There is real value in being able to have a specific list of items that need to be addressed. This not only helps the salesperson to focus but also helps them to return to key points if the conversation gets off of the topic.

"Best practices" for sales calling scheduling looks like this:

The salesperson has "real" appointments, including specific call objectives—agreed to by the customer

The day before every sales call, the salesperson e-mails (faxes in the old days) the agenda to the customer—confirming the call and reminding the customer of the agreed-upon items to be discussed. The combination of a well-set-up sales call with a professional reminder is a powerful tool that not only increases the chances of success (and the likelihood that the customer will actually be there for the call), but also dramatically increases the salesperson's professionalism in the mind of the customer. (Remember that follow-up skills was identified as one of the key values added by a salesperson. This approach demonstrates follow-up ability in advance of actually getting of an order.)

Assemble what is needed

Before the day begins (ideally late afternoon of the day before), professional salespeople (inside or outside) review the calls planned for the next day and then put together what they need. There are few things that hurt the image of a salesperson worse than getting out on a call and then not providing something that they said they would provide. If a salesperson cannot be counted on to even bring what they need to a call, the customer has a hard time thinking they can depend on them (and their organization) when it comes to something important…like an order.

Summary

Professional selling requires professional preparation. Help the salespeople to be better prepared by reviewing the following:

What does the salesperson want to accomplish?
Does the salesperson understand the value to the customer?
Do they review their account knowledge before trying to schedule the call?
Are they scheduling "real" sales calls?
Do they use written call plans?
Do they have what they will need to complete the call objectives?

Section 7.3 The Sales Call

Part of the sales management job is to observe sales calls: in person and on the phone.

As a manager, there are several specific things that you should look for when you are making joint calls with salespeople:

Number of "sales" calls
Call schedule
Call plans
Call quality
Penetration
Personal attributes
Sales mechanics

Number of "sales" calls: Your first assessment relates to the call plans. Look at the calls the salesperson is going to make. Review the written call plans (or mental call plans if that's what you have to deal with.) How many of the calls do you regard as true "sales" calls versus "service" calls? Your first definition is that if most of the items on the call plan are "service" issues, it would be regarded as a service call.

And, are these the right calls? A lot of sales managers focus on the "mechanics" of the call to the detriment of the sales process. This is an example of not seeing the forest for the trees. Making a good call on the wrong customer is not really a good call at all. Make sure that you not only look at what happens on the call but whether the call should have taken place at all.

Call schedule: One of the things for you to look for is the call scheduling behavior. Many salespeople have some very bad habits—no calls scheduled on Monday mornings and Friday afternoons; no calls scheduled before 9:00 or after 3:30; no lunch meetings or breakfast meetings with customers; and no appointments several days before or after holidays. The assumption is that people do not want to see salespeople at those times—this is only true if the salesperson adds no value.

As a manager, you want to work with your salespeople to maximize the amount of their day that they spend actually talking to customers. (It would be even nicer if they were trying to sell them something but face/phone time is the first step.) Do they spend too much time in the office—not selling? When you work with salespeople, see what time they make the first call and the last call. You might also want to spend some Mondays, Fridays and time around holidays to see what happens on those kinds of days, as well. And also flip through their calendars and see what they have been doing and what they plan to do, going forward.

<u>Call Plans:</u> We have spoken about written call plans. Ask the salesperson to show you their objectives for each call. Can they show you or do they have to tell you?

<u>Call quality:</u> There are four things that are critically important in improving call quality. The first is punctuality. If the call was scheduled for 10:00, when did the salesperson call or show up? Punctuality is one of the things that distinguishes the great ones from the average ones. The attitude of the salesperson towards time also sends a message to the customer. When our salesperson is late, it not only sends a message of disrespect to the customer but also gives the customer permission to be cavalier with the salesperson's time from them on.

As an aside, this is one of the reasons why some salespeople do not want to set firm appointments. They do not think they can be on time so they are deliberately vague about appointments. But it is better to set firm appointments—and make them—than to have squishy appointments.

Pay attention to is whether the salesperson followed the call plan. When I get a verbal call plan I always write it down and then show the salesperson the things they said they were going to address that they did not deal with. You want to get your salespeople to start thinking about the order of things—which things should we discuss first? And the importance of following the plan they established.

The third call quality issue involves the accomplishment of the objectives. The salesperson may have discussed them, but did they actually accomplish them. For example, if the salesperson's objective was to get an opportunity to quote XYZ and it was discussed but the customer did not allow us to quote it, then we really did not accomplish our objective. How many of the things the salesperson said they were going to accomplish did they actually accomplish on the call?

The final issue is that on every point discussed the salesperson needs to define the next step and get the customer to agree. Of all the "tricks" in sales, this is one that really does work. If the salesperson discusses a piece of business and leaves it open, there is a good chance that it will not turn into an order. The same goes for "telling" the customer what is going to happen next. The salesperson can tell the customer they will call them next Tuesday to get a list of items to quote but it is much stronger if the salesperson "asks" when it would be convenient to call and get the list. Then the customer has a stake in moving the business along.

Account penetration: The phrase, "It's not what you know, it's who you know," is still a valid part of the sales lexicon. This is especially true when organizations are in transition. How are decisions being made in your industry? More committees, more input from users, more oversight from upper management? If so, you need to pay attention to "who" the salesperson knows (and calls on) in the accounts. The account profile will help to identify the "who" but the sales call itself is indicative of the actual activity. For example, the salesperson may have twelve names in the account profile but only call on the same two purchasing people every time. Look for problems in the sales arena because either the salesperson does not have the right contacts—not wide enough or strategic enough or because they only call on a limited spectrum of their contacts within a given account. (As an example, some salespeople have upper management contacts but are hesitant to call on them because they are not sure how to make effective calls at that level.)

Sales Mechanics: At last, we are **at home** for many sales managers. This is the part of sales management that most sales managers are good at. This involves the historical sales processes listed below:

Opening
Presentation
Questioning
Listening
Overcoming objections
Closing

Opening—How does the salesperson open the call? Is it appropriate?

Presentation—If they made a presentation, how well did they do it?

Questioning—My recommendation is that you spend a lot of time on this one. Mind control in any conversation comes through questions. When the salesperson asks a question, they force the customer to think about what they want them to think about.

A series of well-constructed questions—in the right order—can help the customer move from apathy to enthusiasm about your product or service. Many salespeople, however, simply wing it when it comes to questions. Many salespeople also do not use open versus closed-ended questions correctly.

Open-ended questions are good for gathering information and getting the customer to open up their minds. An example would be, "What are the most important things your organization has to accomplish this year?"

Closed-ended questions are good for getting agreement, finding problems and closing sales. An example would be, "So the only problem you have with our widget is the color?" This requires a "Yes" or "No" answer and either answer will move you closer to an ultimate "Yes" or "No."

A final word about questions: When your salespeople ask questions, they should have a pretty good idea what the answer will be. If they are ever shocked by an answer, it means that they have not done part of the job of a professional salesperson. This is especially true of the final question, "Can I have the order?"

Listening—Many salespeople do not listen or take notes well. On each call you should write down the important things said by the customer and at the end of the day, you should ask questions and then get the salesperson to show you those answers in their notes. (And, if any of you have been taught that it is rude to take notes on a sales call, unlearn that nonsense. Get your people to listen and take good notes.)

Overcoming objections—Did the salesperson hear the objections when they were offered? Did they respond to them?

Closing—Did the salesperson do the appropriate trial closes? Did they try to close the sale (if they are at the right stage of the sales process?)

Personal Attributes: The final thing for you to consider while observing the sales call is the salesperson. In today's world, there are a lot of things that the salesperson can do to make selling a lot harder. Inappropriate comments, inappropriate dress and grooming are among the top issues to pay attention to.

All comments that demean groups of people are no-nos. Even among customer friends, this is not a good idea. Political and religions discussions are also probably not a good idea unless you are very knowledgeable of your audience.

A lot of organizations have gone casual. While I am not an advocate of three-piece suits for salespeople, I do believe in presenting a professional image. This means that your sales team should dress a half-step above most of the people they are calling on. So if they are calling on people who wear work clothes, the sales team should wear nice slacks and a professional shirt (maybe not a golf shirt). And no matter who they normally call on, they might want to keep a tie (if male) and jacket (both genders) in their vehicle because you never know when someone might drag you into a meeting with the top people and its nice to feel appropriately dressed.

It's also good to be appropriately groomed. Neat is the word, here. No problem on facial hair but people should comb their hair, wear unwrinkled clothes and present a generally neat appearance. (You only do have that one chance to make a good first impression.)

These all apply to inside people, as well. Whenever I work with a team, its almost invariably true that the inside folks that take some pride in how they present themselves to the world just seem to project better through the phone.

Summary

Since the sales call is the part of the process where the customer gets most of the value from the sales process (if done correctly), you want to check on the following:

Does the salesperson have "real" sales calls? Are they on the right customers?
Are they spending sales time making sales calls or doing service activities?
How are they doing on the "quality" issues:

Punctuality?
Following the plan?
Accomplishing objectives?
Defining the next step?

Are they calling on enough of the right people on the call?
How do they do on the "mechanics?"
Do they need to work on the personal attributes?

Section 7.4 Follow-up Activities

Your salesperson has just made a call—good, bad or indifferent. It might have been on the phone or it might have been in person. Both of you are probably in a hurry to get to the next call. The tendency is for the salesperson to move on. But wait, are there things that you want the salesperson to do immediately after the call? Are there some things that lose their value if they are delayed?

The time immediately after a sales call is very important and sales managers should pay attention to the salesperson's post-call activities. There are several items that the most effective professional salespeople do regularly:

Update account profile
Write call report
Update opportunity tracker
Update calendar
Written feedback to customer

Update account profile: If the salesperson is not actually updating the account profile during the call, the most effective time is immediately after the call. Normally, there will only be one or two items that need to be noted such as changes of key personnel or significant shifts in goals or strategies. If this is done immediately after the call, most of the vital information is recorded—otherwise a lot of it is lost.

Write call report: Your author is not a big believer in call reports and his grumpiness will be explained in the section that details sales reporting. But if the salesperson is asked to write call reports, the time to do them is immediately after the call—or at worst at the end of the day. A call report that is written after dinner on the day of the call tends to be less accurate than those written immediately and call reports written at the end of the week assume a sort of vanilla flavoring where only the negatives remain.

Update opportunity tracker: Many organizations are moving toward opportunity management and this is a move that I strongly support. Again, this will be explained in more detail later but the basic thrust is that the only thing that sales management must have is a clear picture of the sales opportunities that are on-going. There are many systems that allow the salesperson to provide good reporting without taking a lot of time—and if these systems are in place in your organization, they should be filled out immediately after the call.

Update calendar: To be a professional salesperson you have to have a calendar—that is with you at all times. Remember that the most important element of selling is to move each opportunity as far along as possible on each sales call. This does not mean that every call will end in a closing attempt only that the salesperson will move as far as possible on each call. This requires the use of a calendar because the most valuable form of moving a sale along is to schedule the next step with the customer and this requires a calendar—and an immediate update of all the required activities after each sales call.

Written feedback to customer: The most professional salespeople have a habit of documenting what has been discussed during a sales call and sending it to the customer. Again the best time to do this is immediately after the call but sometimes it's okay to do it at the end of the day. Think of the image that your sales team would present if the customer received a summary of the call and also received a confirming agenda in advance of every call. Compare those professional behaviors to those of your competition and your people look like winners even when they are not in front of the customer.

These summaries also prove to be very valuable in today's climate when multiple people are involved in decisions. If you are meeting with one member of the team (but do not see all team members on that call), a memo that summarizes what happened not only makes your salesperson look more professional but also keeps other team members up to date—and more likely to support your salesperson in the future. (This is especially true when your people are calling on technical people. A good approach would be to always send a summary of your conversations to the purchasing people that might ultimately be placing the orders—even if they do not make the decisions.)

Thank the customer. It's been written (and said) a lot over the years but "Thanks" is a neglected form of compensation. We've mentioned it before but in a real sales situation—where your salesperson is attempting to convince the customer to either buy something from you they have never bought before or to buy something from you for the first time (replacing an existing supplier), there is a hidden personal risk to the people who have to make that decision. The risk is that when they switch you will screw up and they will look bad. One way to make it easier for people to take that risk is to thank them. If you thank them for seeing you, thank you for giving them an opportunity to work on a project, thank them for an opportunity to present a quote or proposal—it's more likely that the salesperson will get to thank them for the ultimate—an order.

A sincere written "thank you" is a seldom used and very effective weapon in a salesperson's bag.

<u>Summary</u>

As you can see, there are many specific items for the sales manager to pay attention to when working with salespeople in the field. These issues are addressed in more detail in the section dealing with joint calls (and we have even provided a joint call review form for use by the sales manager). The value added by a sales manager, however, is the ability to not be concerned as much with the individual opportunity as to the approach that the salesperson takes. Is the salesperson doing the right things? Are they being done consistently? Are the results the ones that are desired?

If not, the sales manager can intervene by either getting the salesperson to do something they do not do, getting them to something more often or getting them to do something differently. Apply this checklist to the salespeople and see how well they measure up on the their calls.

What does the salesperson do immediately after the call? Are they putting off until tomorrow something that would be done much better today?

Sales Management Self-Audit

Rate each answer on a scale of 1-10 with 1 being "Not at all" and 10 being "Totally."

We have a sales management process to monitor the following:

_____Method for setting calls.
_____Sales call problems.

Preparation issues, such as:
_____Account information reviews.
_____Call plans.

Call issues, such as:
_____"Real" sales calls on the right customers.
_____Use of sales time.
_____Call mechanics.
_____Personal attributes.

Follow-up issues, such as:
_____Appropriate documentation
_____Appropriate customer interaction

Add your numbers and give yourself a score: _____. (Add back nothing this time. The author giveth and he taketh away.)

Section 8.0 Sales Management Tools

Throughout this work, we have talked about the different aspects of sales and specifically how sales management can impact the behaviors and results of each part of the process. In this section, we are going to review the tools that are identified as sales management tools. The discussion will identify the tool, how it may be used and when to use it. Many of you are having fantasies about blunt instruments right about now and, in fact, many of the things described in this section have just about that impact on your sales team—or at least on specific members of your sales team.

One of your challenges is to have the tools you need—and to use them to get more (or less) of certain activities or results. This means that each tool should only be used a certain way—in specific situations. Unfortunately, many sales organizations have a whole raft of tools in place—each created to serve a purpose that may not now be valid.

Our first recommended activity is for you to take stock of the current management tools now in place in your organization (and how they are used). We are defining management tools in the following general areas:

Account profiles. (Sounds like reporting but this is more than a reporting tool, if used appropriately, so it will be discussed separately.)

Calendars/itineraries. (These are two separate tools—each has a different purpose.)

Joint calls. (These are defined as calls a manager makes for the purpose of managing. This does not cover the times when the manager goes into the field to address a particular issue at a customer.)

Meetings. (There are different kinds of sales meetings—held at different times—with different agendas.)

Reporting. (There are a lot of different kinds of reports as well as different uses for reports. This section includes my heretical rantings against call reports—and a judicious discussion of how and when to use them.)

Sales Force Automation. (An overview of some of the "whys" and "wherefores" of automating some of the functions above.)

Sales Force Measurements. (A list of specific measurements that are useful to sales managers—and how to use them.)

Section 8.1 Overview

There are a series of things to consider before implementing any tool. The first is:

What is the value to me of this particular tool?

Before implementing any sales management tool, you should be able to define very clearly the exact benefits that you get. For example, "If we implement account profiles, I can quickly determine (without a laborious, time-consuming interview process) everything that I need to know about the salesperson's knowledge of the customer," or "If we implement an account profile system, I can eliminate four days a year worth of meetings that were used to educate me about what the salespeople knew about their customers."

These are pretty good benefit statements because they define specific reasons to implement the tool and a benefit: four additional days of your time that can be spent on more beneficial activities than having the sales team regurgitate what they already know.

The second question that you need to ask yourself is: How often do I need to use the tool? A good example of this would be sales meetings. Some organizations have weekly sales meetings, some monthly, some quarterly and some just have an annual meeting.

Why? Is weekly too often or not enough? (There are certain businesses and business conditions that might require a daily meeting to check on progress.) Is an annual meeting really enough?

The same holds true for all of the tools that will be discussed. Unfortunately, many of you inherited systems which require certain things at certain times. Make sure that the reasons (and timing) are still valid.

The next question involves feedback. How often will you provide feedback on a certain tool? Call reports are an excellent example. If you ask for them on a weekly basis, how often do you need to provide feedback on what you have seen? You guessed it, weekly. If a salesperson submits a call report and they do not hear back from their manager, the assumption is that you have not read it. One time I submitted the exact same call reports (although not in the same order) for four weeks in a row and never heard anything from my manager. That proved to me that they were not really important. How many messages like that are you sending to your team in the way in which you treat your management tools? How important are those sales meetings, really, when you frequently reschedule them or skip them because of something that has come up on your end?

One of the most important things to consider about the use of any tool is that there are different ways to present them to your team. The main way that tools are presented is that the manager mandates the use of something—"From now on, we're going to use this call planning format," would be an example of this approach.

But most sales managers also recognize that mandating the use of something is only part of the battle. How many times do you have to follow up with a salesperson to get them to turn in a call report or even an expense report for which they are reimbursed? The general perception is that salespeople do not like paperwork and while this is probably true at some level, part of the problem is that salespeople are asked to fill out more reports than almost anyone else in the organization. Think about it this way, how many call reports is the purchasing agent asked to fill out? Even the finance people who compile reports are almost never asked to fill out reports on their activities.

So while part of the issue may be one of reluctance, the main issue with many sales management tools is that the salespeople often see no benefit (to them or their organization) in participating.

So before implementing a tool, of any kind, you might want to consider the following question:

What's in it for the salesperson?

Let's use the example of call reports. Construct an argument of the value of submitting a call report for the salesperson. You have 30 seconds. Time's up. How did you do?

A lot of people answer this question with a flip comment such as, "They get to keep their job." (This is not always perceived as a benefit, by the way.) Worse, still, it does not really get at the real reason and 'it's often not true. How many good salespeople have been fired because of refusal to submit call reports (on time?)

Whenever someone is confronted with the request to do an activity, there is a response that is driven by one of two key thought processes—does this get me closer to what I want? Or what is the pain level if I do not do it? A great many salespeople are not primarily motivated to do things by avoiding pain. A great many are motivated by what they can get to by doing a certain activity. Yet, the assumption of many sales managers is that they should do these things to avoid pain—such as management displeasure or withheld travel reimbursements.

So taking our example above, the value to a salesperson of submitting call reports are potentially as follows:

A formal written record of what is happening in the account (that supplements the account profile) that allows the salesperson to keep on track of key business opportunities; or

A tool that allows them to determine if there are territory-wide or customer segment trends that they might be able to exploit for more business or might warn them of some impending difficulties before they become acute.

If the salesperson values either one of these, they would be more inclined to do call reports.

Just keep this exercise in mind as you consider using the sales management tools detailed in this section. Sometimes you can "tell" and sometimes you need to "sell." Whenever you ask someone to modify their behaviors, you might want to remember that the question they always ask (although sometimes not out loud) is, What's in it for me?

You should at least try to answer that question before implementing any sales management tool.

Section 8.2 Account Profiles

Account profiles can be used in several different ways. The first question that you need to consider is: What problem are you trying to solve? Are you concerned about the quality of your prospecting effort? Concerned about the level of account penetration? Not certain whether we are calling on the right people? All of these are valid concerns of sales management and an account profile can provide you with a quick diagnostic tool—as well as a development tool that can drive improvement. (Don't confuse this with a marketing tool. You can use it to gather market information but the real value is as a sales management tool.)

If you are considering implementing account profiles or if you have one and are not getting a lot of buy-in, consider the question: What's the value to the salesperson?

There is probably a correlation between the people in your organization that know the most about their accounts and their income. Maybe you should document this correlation and share it with your team. What are the other reasons why your salespeople should value using an account profile?

Account Profile Defined

An account profile is a collection of information about prospects and customers. It is a living document—meaning that a profile is never "complete" because the learning process should never stop. Account profiles seek to collect data in three main areas:

What the salesperson needs to know about the organization

What the salesperson needs to know about the specific applications where they can sell their product/service

What the salesperson needs to know about the decision-making process within the organization and the people involved in it

The organization

What do your salespeople need to know about each of their customers to sell them? To sell them more effectively?

I have already presented some of the basics:

Market segment: Are they in a segment that is growing, shrinking, moving to China?

Size of organization: Which buying influences are at this location? Are they large enough to justify significant sales effort?

Organizational goals: Who is their competition? What are their competitive issues?

What are their major goals for the year? What is their vision for the future of their organization?

Potential: If we sold them everything we could sell them, how much is it?

At a minimum, the salesperson should know all of these items because this gives them the insights that they need to be able to link what they want to sell into the customer's needs.

Each selling situation is different so one of your primary jobs as a manager is to define what they need to know. What are the additional things that might be helpful?

The application

Understanding the organization is just part of the knowledge needed to sell. The area that most salespeople focus on is the application. The salesperson has to identify a specific need within the organization. Are they designing a new product? Are they re-engineering an existing product—to reduce cost? To enhance features? To improve manufacturing efficiencies? To reduce inventory? Are they opening a new facility? Retro-fitting an existing facility? Closing the facility to do preventative maintenance?

A sales professional needs to understand all of these issues and be able to document the conditions that surround an opportunity. (Some of this knowledge may be more appropriate for call reports or opportunity management buy it may also be included in the account profile data.)

As with the organization, your salespeople need to know several specific pieces of information about the application. As a manager, your goal is to create a few questions to ask the salespeople that will help you to understand if they have sufficient knowledge for each piece of business they are working on.

The Decision-Making Process

We have addressed this issue previously. This part of the account profile is the one that is most often included. Most account profiles have places where people can list their contacts and the job titles and ways to get in touch with them—phone numbers, e-mail addresses and shipping addresses.

In the old days, there were also a lot of account profiles that included places to record their customer's hobbies, birthdays, anniversaries, spouse's names and a lot of other information designed to drive the "personal" side of sales. Without completely dismissing the value of some of those questions, I would recommend that you de-emphasize it. Some of your customers will not like these kinds of questions and others will not be influenced by them—but you know best for your selling situation, so keep what you think is right.

The most important thing for the sales manager to pay attention to in this portion of the profile is, "Is the salesperson calling on the right people?" (Remember the discussion on TAC vs PUC and part of the process—Trigger, Design, Purchasing or Order—you want to focus on.)

Who tend to be the "real" decision-makers and influencers for what we are trying to sell? Has your salesperson identified them on their account profile? Do we have enough technical names? Do we have enough management names? Are we touching all the bases or is the salesperson's contact limited to some low level people that are easy to see?

What are the things that you think the salesperson needs to know about the way decisions are made and the people involved?

How to use them

If you do not have account profiles, you should begin using them—for key customers, at least. Once you have them, use them in the following ways:

As an aid in prospecting
As an aid in call preparation
As an aid in problem-solving
As an aid in driving account contact

Prospecting: If your organization has a goal of getting new customers, you have already established a formal target customer list. One way of ensuring that progress is being made on this list is use the account profile as an assignment. For example, you might ask the salesperson to conduct four survey calls and ask them to give you copies of the account profiles after each call. This will allow you to follow-up on prospecting activity without sounding like this, "Have you made your prospecting calls?"

You can also see patterns in the account profiles. What kind of names does the salesperson find early in the prospecting process? What do they always find out? What do they never find out?

This simple analysis will not only let you know if prospecting activity is occurring but also the quality of the activity—and it will provide you with guidance on what you need to do to help the salesperson improve—if improvement is needed.

Call preparation: Before making calls with a salesperson, you should always ask to review the profiles for the customers/prospects that the two of you are going to call on. This review signifies the importance you place on preparation. You can also use the profiles as part of the review prior to an important call the salesperson is going to make without you. Review what they know—and what they don't know and help them to see the importance of good account knowledge prior to making important (all) calls.

Problem-solving: Many times when a salesperson is having difficulty selling an account, it's because they do not know enough about it to sell it. If a salesperson is having difficulty, ask them to make a presentation to you about what they know. Ask them for their records. Are they trying to remember key things about a customer? Are there a lot of things they do not know? In one example, the salesperson was supposed to get design wins but over 85% of their listed contacts were in purchasing. The problem is obvious.

Account contact: Account profiles also give you insight into how frequently a salesperson calls on an account. (Several of my customers use automated systems that print out a list of account profiles that have not been updated in 30 days. If a key customer or prospect shows up on that report, it's an indication that they are either not making enough contact or not making the kinds of calls where they are learning anything). Some of you might be thinking that the salespeople are just not filling in the information and you might be right about that—but that's another kind of management problem, isn't it?

Note that the account profile is not just a diagnostic tool—as described above, but also a development tool. The act of assigning an account profile and working with the salesperson to improve quality allows you to help them get better.

The most important thing for you to keep in mind about account profiles is that you should not use them as punishment—and you should not use them to gather reams of information that no one uses. A lot of organizations put questions in there to help them understand the market—thereby converting salespeople into market research people. This may be important but be careful about what you ask for, you may get more of it than you want.

Another common mistake is to ask for account profile data and then never provide feedback on what you get. If you ask for it, make sure that you monitor it and provide feedback—otherwise you are sending the message that this is just another useless bit of paperwork.

Section 8.3 Calendars/Itineraries

The only thing that a salesperson really has to sell is their time. This time can be spent in a variety of ways:

Solving service issues such as billing errors, missed shipments or quality issues

Providing technical support
Building relationships with individuals
Making deliveries
Traveling
Writing reports
Or…

Selling

Even if most of their time is spent selling, they can still spend it incorrectly:

Working with the wrong customers
Working with the wrong people within customers
Working on the wrong opportunities
Working on things that are not opportunities at all

As a manager, part of your time should be spent helping your people to focus on doing the right things—especially during prime selling time. If you have done a good job of directing the sales effort (see the sections on strategy and planning), your salespeople have a clear picture of what they should be doing. But even people that know what they should be doing often don't do it. (You and I should be at the gym right now, right?)

So your efforts need to be directed to both understanding how your salespeople are spending their time—and tweaking their schedules—in advance—when you see a problem. This is the real value of calendars and itineraries.

Consider the question: What problem do we want to solve?

This tool can help you identify and correct the following—not enough calls; not enough calls on the right customers; not enough calls on the right people; and not enough calls to sell the things you want them to sell. (You might even get some insight into the reality of individual pieces of business.)

What's in it for the salesperson? Professional salespeople use calendars. In keeping with my theme of not recommending specific products, I will not make a recommendation here but every salesperson needs a calendar because it is the ultimate time management tool. Most of the salespeople that earn in excess of $100,000 in commission are almost religious in their calendar use.

Effective use does not necessarily include any of the hand-held devices or expensive pre-lined paper but it does involve a discipline. A salesperson who occasionally uses a calendar has about the same impact as a couple that occasionally uses birth control.

Calendars

A calendar is the salesperson' basic tool. They use it to keep up with what they are committed to do. As a manager, you can use the tool to help you do your job. This can be done either formally or informally. At times, you can simply do an occasional review of a salesperson's calendar. For example, I review them every time I spend time working with a salesperson. Before the day begins, I ask permission to glance through them to see what has been scheduled, what is scheduled for the current week and what is scheduled over the next few weeks. (If you remember our discussion on always scheduling the next step, you can see how a forward looking calendar review will provide valuable insight. What if your salesperson has nothing scheduled beyond this week? That's a pretty good indication that they are making little or no attempt to build sales momentum but are simply living one week at a time.)

This kind of review is informal. There is no set time when the calendars are due.

A second step is ask to see the calendars on a regular basis. Sometimes, I ask every salesperson to fax, e-mail or copy me on their calendars on a weekly basis. This will tell me some things—but not everything that I might need to know about the planned activities of the sales force.

When you do review calendars, look for the following:

Are there any appointments scheduled, at all? Some salespeople only have scheduled dental appointments—and this does not count. A calendar page that says, for example, May 12 and has Des Moines with a line drawn down the page indicates where the salesperson intends to be—but not that any appointments are scheduled.

If appointments are scheduled, are there enough of them? I am not an advocate of setting a target of 20 calls per week, for example, because there may be times when that kind of order is counter-productive. But you should give each salesperson an average of how many appointments you expect in a week—an example might be 12-15. If they fail to hit it once in a while, no problem, but if they fail to hit it several weeks in a row, you may have a problem of some sort. (The problem might be that you do not understand the dynamics of the territory-so keep that in mind-but if the salesperson has been hitting the target and then does not—for a while—something is going on there.)

Remember, also, to look for patterns of unscheduled time. Are they routinely giving up almost all Monday mornings, Friday afternoons, or lunch times? If so, you might point this out to them with an eye for future improvements.

If enough appointments are scheduled, are they on the right customers? You created a strategy and a sales plan was designed to focus your sales team on certain customers or customer segments—are they calling on them? A salesperson can make a lot of calls on the wrong customers—to satisfy your quota requirements.

Again, if your salespeople have an occasional week where they do not hit the right customers, that may be ok, but if it is a recurring action, you might have a problem. Pay attention to the patterns—and changes in patterns.

If they have enough appointments scheduled on the right customers, are they calling on the right people? (Since a real appointment has a person's name attached to it, you can see this at a glance, right?) If you look at a calendar and you see the same person's name every time and you know that there are five or six other people in that organization that they should be seeing, again, you might have a problem.

If they have enough appointments on the right customers and they appear to be calling on the right people, are they talking about the right things? This one is a little harder to understand because very few salespeople list the topics of discussion in their calendar. Remember that our definition of a real sales appointment included a topic agreed to by the customer. (Of course, if you think you might have a problem with this with a particular salesperson, you might give them a calendar form that has a place to write the topics down, right?)

Otherwise, you have to resort to the laborious process of asking them what they intend to talk about. (That is, unless you decide to do some sort of opportunity tracking—which we will discuss later).

Whatever you decide to do, this is an important part of sales management because many salespeople fail because they are not trying to do the right things so even if they are successful in doing what they are

LONG!

attempting to do, it does not meet your definition of success.

Itineraries

A calendar is a tool carried by the salesperson. You can look backwards and forwards in a calendar. An itinerary is a more focused tool which can be simply a page of a salesperson's calendar faxed (e-mailed) to you on a weekly basis or a different document that you ask them to fill out.

An itinerary is normally expected by close of business on Friday and is a detailed look at what the salesperson intends to do next week. (This is a good tool to use if you are trying to break salespeople from setting appointments on Monday mornings.)

The value of an itinerary (rather than the more random looks talked about above) is that it allows the sales manager to have a regular impact on the sales activities—before they occur.

As an example, if you ask your salespeople to submit an itinerary every Friday afternoon by 4:00 pm that details the appointments, by individual—including job title and the topics to be discussed, you can review them and make suggested changes before the week begins. Take Salesperson Jones whose itinerary shows only three calls scheduled on his top 20 customers, all on purchasing people and most without any mention of the new product you want him to focus on. You can call, fax, e-mail or confront in person this plan and maybe get some of the activities changed—now!!!

One of the indictments I have against a lot of reporting is that there is very little that can be done about it except to maybe correct it before it happens again. With itineraries, however, you can correct the mistakes before they occur.

A variation on this theme is to ask salespeople to submit two documents every Friday afternoon—their plan for next week and their current week's plan with an indication of what really occurred. (One time when I was managing a group of salespeople I noticed that the call reports did not seem to link up with the scheduled appointments so I used this document to show the salesperson that they were not really working their own plan.)

Itineraries are more paperwork-intensive than calendars because the salesperson has to fill them out. But if you have concerns about your ability to impact future behaviors, this sales management tool might be the answer.

Section 8.4 Joint Calls

Some of the most fun we have as sales managers is the joint call. The open road, the fresh air, the joyous smiles of the customers as we visit them...

Regardless of whether we like to make them or not, joint calls are an important sales management tool. Unfortunately, many sales managers do not make good ones. The tendency is for salespeople to use managers to make difficult calls for them—or the sales manager decides to take the calls over and just do the job whether the salesperson wants them to or not. In this case you are not the national sales manager but the national salesman or woman.

The purpose of making these calls (except for specific calls where you are there to be bludgeoned) is to see what happens on a regular basis. You will never see this if every time you travel you actually do the calls.

Consider the kinds of problems you might like to address with joint sales calls:

Are they calling on the right kinds of customers?
Are they calling on the right people?
Do they have solid relationships?
Are they talking about the right things?
Are their sales mechanics (probing, questioning, listening, closing skills) good?

We discussed some of these things earlier in the section dealing with sales calls.

(You will probably not get much insight into issues such as the number of sales calls they normally make using this tool. I've heard salespeople say that when their managers travel with them, they start with a 6:00 am breakfast and conclude with a dinner meeting just so the manager thinks they work like that every day. The calendar/call reports will provide more insight into this question than a field day.)

What's in it for the salespeople? Some professional critique of their performance—which they should welcome. Some new ideas to get around problems. Maybe even seeing a few tricks performed—if you know how to perform them.

The following should be elements of your process for making joint calls with your sales team.

<u>Setting a call schedule</u>

The first thing that you need to do is to decide the percent of your time that you intend to spend making joint calls. If you have a veteran sales team that is providing the results you want, you might spend as little as a day a quarter out in the field with each member of the team. If you have a rookie sales team, you might have to spend three days a week out in the field. And if you are unlucky enough to be the sales manager/Field Applications Engineer, you might spend almost every day in the field. This is your first consideration:

Based on the needs of the sales team, how much time do you need to spend working with the team.

I also saved one little bombshell that I will proceed to drop on you now—part of your joint call time needs to be devoted to your inside sales team, customer service people and your technical support staff, if you have one. If these people report to you (and they have on-going customer contact), you need to see what happens. This means that part of your ride-along sales time is really sit-along sales time—and this is hard to do but essential. On numerous occasions, I have been told how inside sales or customer service behaves by management. But when I sit with them, I get a different story. One sales manager told me that every time a customer called in to request Item A, the inside salesperson asked them if they wanted to buy Item B. In my two hours of observing, I documented 17 cases where that did not occur. Don't underestimate your need for spending time with these people.

After you have decided how much of your time you intend to spend in the field, decide how much time you intend to spend with each salesperson and let them know it. It's perfectly OK to spend one day per quarter with one salesperson and one day a week with another. Budget the time you need to work with the people that need it. (If you look at it this way, one of the rewards of being a professional is that they do not have to spend much time with you! Of course, even the veterans need some time so no one gets off without some joint calls.)

You have a choice of telling the salesperson in advance that you intend to work with them on Tuesday or just showing up in the morning with your best customer smile on and doing it. If you tell them in advance you are sending one message, if you just show up, you might be sending them a message that you are not sure if they are always accurate with their calendars. Just be aware that the way you do it sends a message.

Beware of salespeople that ask you what kind of calls you want to make when you work with them. My answer is, "I just want to see what you planned to do on Tuesday." If you tell them what you want to see, you are actually taking responsibility for the day and that's a no-no. Also beware of making the same calls over and over. A lot of salespeople only take their managers to places where they are well-received. If this occurs, its perfectly ok to tell the salesperson that you want to see some new customers this time.

Having a plan

When you observe, you should have some specific things you are looking for with each salesperson. If you go into the field without an emphasis, you are doing both of you a disservice. This does not mean that you are not supposed to notice things that go wrong but you should focus on one or two items at a time. Before you go out, be clear on what you are looking for.

Preparation

Assuming that you let them know you were going to ride with them, meet them in advance and go over things that are important such as their calendars, their profiles, their calls plans, etc. If you use your time with them to reinforce the value of the sales tools, they are more likely to use the tools when you are not there.

During the call

This is the hard part of being a sales manager. Unless you are there to solve a problem you should really stay pretty quiet during the day. I know that you will be bursting with great things to say to the customer but you are out there to hear what the salesperson says, right? So after exchanging polite greetings, just sit back and let the brilliance of your sales team wash over you. (This does not apply to multi-million dollar opportunities about to go south—in that case fight as valiantly as you can to save it, but you get the point. For the most part, be silent and observe.)

Take lots of notes. Pay attention to what the customer says that is truly important and the specifics of what the salesperson did and said. When you debrief, specific examples are much more powerful than general statements—plus this will give you an opportunity to show off your note-taking skills.

Do not lay your critique out in small pieces throughout the day. Make notes to yourself and present them once at the end of the day.

Providing critique

One of the reasons why salespeople hate these little visits is because most critique is negative. Therefore, it's probably a good idea to provide positive feedback first, if there is any. And limit your critique to three things, max. You may have found 23 items that really needed attention but if you lay them all out, the salesperson will become more and more defensive and be unable to deal with it. So pick what is most important and get improvement there.

My recommendation is for you to use some sort of written critique sheet (an example is provided) and for you to provide the salesperson with a specific written list of positive/negative comments. In this way, there is no confusion about what is important and the salesperson is very clear on what is important to work on.

Part of being a good manager is to provide some specific guidance on what you want people to improve—and some ways of measuring that improvement. If you are not happy with the salesperson's skills, you need to tell them how you both will know that they are improved. For instance, if you are unhappy with the quality of the people the salesperson is calling on, you might say something like, "The next time we work together I would like to see at least one call on management out of three— rather than what we did today."

An answer from you that sounds like, "I'll know it when I see it," is worthless and counter-productive. If you can't explain the improvement you want, wait until you can figure out what you want before you give the critique.

Following up

Each time you work with a salesperson, you need to put a copy of your notes into some sort of file with that salesperson's name on it. It could be a file folder on your hard drive or it could be a three-hole punched sheet of paper that goes into a notebook behind each salesperson's name. Either way, your goal is to keep a written record of your visits. This serves two purposes:

You will be able to review the notebook before working with the salesperson next time so that you are providing consistent critique rather than starting from scratch every time.

These comments will be invaluable to you when you do the annual performance review and development plan which we will discuss in the next section.

Section 8.5 Sales Meetings

You may not regard sales meetings as a management tool but they can be. A meeting can be whatever you want it to be from a form of communication to a team-building exercise and everything in between. As a manager, your job is to be clear on what you want your meetings to do—and then structure them so that you get what you need.

What kinds of problems do you want to solve? Is the purpose of the meeting to get everyone on the same page, to share information, to build the team concept, to provide training/development opportunities or to assist you in management reporting?

You send a lot of different messages based on the following elements of a meeting:

The frequency of the meetings
The timing
The length
The agenda

It's ok to do more than one thing with your meetings but if you try to do everything with every meeting you end up doing nothing with all meetings. (That was a brilliant thought, I thought.)

And, consider the value to the troops: getting the latest information, opportunity to interact with peers and tips on improving performance all come to mind. Why should your salespeople value your meetings?

The Frequency

The frequency of sales meetings says a lot about how they should be used. A weekly meeting suggests a huge need to check on activities and results. This is normally found in businesses with less-experienced sales people or companies where a lot of things change or where a lot of coordination is required to make things happen. You might be thinking that a weekly meeting is impossible given the dispersion of your sales team but with telephones, I have found that any company can have a weekly meeting—if there is a need.

You might even have different types of meeting at different times—an annual meeting for new product introductions; quarterly meeting where results are reviewed, in detail, and some in-depth training occurs and monthly meetings that are simply results/problem oriented.

The Timing

The timing of your meetings says a lot, as well. A Monday morning conference call that starts at 7:30 sends a different message than a meeting that starts at 9:30. A meeting on Friday afternoon at 4:00 sends a different message than a lunch meeting on Wednesday.

I'm on the fence about weekend meetings. On the one hand, they make a nice statement about the need to sell during sales time but on the other hand, since you are asking people to give up "their" time, you might actually be casting a negative pall over the meeting before it begins. (And I have a real problem about asking people to come in on Saturday mornings in the summer to get sales training.)

The point you need to take away from this is that you should consider the timing of your meetings as part of the message you want to send. The fact that sales meeting have always been Monday morning at 9:30 is not a good reason to keep having them at that time.

The Length

The length of your meetings is something else that should not be left up to chance. If the purpose of the meeting is to review numbers, you keep it to under an hour. If there are other issues that come up, write them down and address them later. A lot of managers are not very good at facilitating meetings and for this reason, a lot of useless conversations go on that only apply to one or two people in the room while everyone else twiddles their thumbs. Show people that time is valuable by keeping this sort of behavior to a minimum.

If you are having a training session (or an annual meeting), fight the desire to start every day at 6:30 am and end every evening at 8:00. I know that the meetings are expensive and you want to pack everything in but the end result is people that are brain dead and stop learning somewhere in the second day (if not the afternoon of the first.)

Probably the most crucial part of meeting length, however, is to start when you say you will and stop when you say you will. This not only shows your concern for time but also builds your credibility.

The Agenda

Ok, some basic meeting rules. Have an agenda, publish it in advance and follow it. Got it? Now, let's talk about some specific things that can (and should) be on a sales meeting agenda. Each one of these can be the purpose for the meeting or a portion of the meeting.

Review of Results versus Plan: Sales meetings should start with some metrics. If you have a weekly meeting, you can do this one monthly but every month you should report on where the organization is—relative to its goals. Further, you might even (gasp!) post results by salesperson in the same way. This sends a different message—and maybe it's a message that some of your people need to hear.

Joseph C. Ellers

Review of sales for focus customers/products/services: If you have dignified certain groups as important, you should report on how those efforts are turning out. Again, you might even consider highlighting the salespeople that have been most effective in achieving the strategic portion of the goals. You send a different message when you highlight the salesperson that sold the most of what we wanted to sell versus the salesperson that sold the most, period.

Product/service presentation by a salesperson: I like to get the salespeople involved in leading portions of the sales meetings. There are many good reasons for this: it helps them to learn if they have to teach, you can critique their presentation if it needs work, and other salespeople learn from "real" experiences. There is also the added benefit of breaking up the monotony of your beautiful voice. One of the reasons why consultants like myself exist—other than our good looks, charm, brilliance and modesty—is that we say things differently. (Don't let the word get out but often we say what you have been saying for years—but because it comes from a different source, it has more validity.) Take advantage of this and get your salespeople to help you sell <u>them</u> on new ideas.

This is also the product/service training piece where you provide knowledge on the "what" we are selling. This piece also could cover new product/service introductions.

Account presentation: Ditto most of the above. If you have a salesperson that is doing well with an account, get them to tell the story to the group. This kind of presentation not only helps you to understand how well a salesperson understands one of their key accounts but also serves to train other salespeople with similar accounts on how to be more effective.

With both of these above, you make it more or less aggressive, depending on how you structure the response. One approach is for you to conduct a brief review of what was learned. The other is to allow the salespeople to critique what was just said. You will get different results based on the approach you use and you will also raise more (or less) fear.

Sales tip: This is your moment to shine. You might present a specific sales topic. Try not to do product/service training but focus on how to sell it— not what it is.

Forecast: You may already require some sort of rolling forecast in your organization. What I am suggesting here is a little more focused. At least once a month, normally at the end, I ask every salesperson to forecast the major pieces of business they will book within the next 30 days, in writing. While this may a valuable tool for the production part of your business, the real value is that it lets you get a great insight into the salesperson's real knowledge of the sales process.

You need to define the kinds of orders they are to forecast and do not let them forecast dollars—but specific pieces of business. You want them to tell you that they intend to book these four pieces of business—then you should track this and let them know how right they were. Some salespeople never get one right for the first few months because they really have no idea where they are in the process or what they need to do next. This little exercise will flesh it out pretty clearly. As an aside, it's pretty hard to forecast something that does not have a scheduled close date (or is not at least very close to being quoted), so pay attention to what they think is closeable business.

Those are some of the things that you can do in your sales meetings. There are lots of others. Just be careful that you do not lose the "sales" part of the meeting in all the other items that crowd their way onto the agenda.

Section 8.6 Sales Reporting

Many of the management tools already discussed are a form of sales reporting. Account profiles and calendars/itineraries are a form of sales reporting as are the monthly forecasts mentioned in the previous section on sales meetings. Each of these has specific uses at specific times. As with every other tool, the key is to begin with the issue that you want sales reporting to address.

Do you want insight into call quality? Do you want to understand what opportunities are being worked? Do you want a temperature check of what is happening in the marketplace? Do you want more market information? All of these are valid requests.

One problem, however, is that many organizations try to cram all of it into one report—the call report. And then the error is compounded by several other things such as:

Management does not enforce the rules evenly
Management does not read the reports
Management does not give feedback on the information
Management (apparently) never uses the information
Management only appears to want the information as a form of checking up (at best) or punishment (at worst)

And when we look at the benefit side, what does the salesperson get out of the call reporting effort? Very little, given the way that most call reports are requested.

I have often described call reports as some the greatest fiction ever written. This comes from reading them for years (and writing a few Pulitzer prize winners, myself—in call report annals, that is.)

So, if you want call reports, begin by defining what you want. Some good uses are listed below:

A list of the calls made and people called on
An opportunity management system
Market information
Customer temperature check

Calls made/people called on: If this is really what you want, maybe an itinerary or even a calendar would suffice. This would take the salesperson a lot less time and would give you a lot of what you are getting out of call reports in an easier-to-read format.

An opportunity management system: If this is really what you want (and I think this is critical), I would like to recommend that you consider using the following format:

Date in	Customer	Contact	Opportunity	Value	Next step	Date

About fifteen years ago, I saw the need for a management tool that had value to everyone, including the salesperson, and I developed a computer program that looked about like this. The key is that the salesperson is only reporting on opportunities—not everything that happens.

To use this format, you would begin by defining the kind of opportunities that you wanted to pay attention to—specific kinds of products/services, specific customers, certain order sizes, etc. This clears away all of the clutter that surrounds a lot of selling activity which is really focused on customer maintenance and not growth.

With that established, we can just look at each line as an opportunity.

The first box is the Date In box. This is the date that the opportunity was found—not the date the call was made. This date can never be changed and will let you (and the salesperson) know how old the opportunity is.

The second box is the Customer box and this lets you know if they are finding opportunities at the right customers. The third box is the Contact box and this allows you to see if the key contact is the right person. The next box is the Opportunity box and this could be a short description or something as simple as a product name. This will allow you to see if the salesperson is working on the right things. The next box is the Value box which lets you keep track of the amount of business they have working. (Its pretty easy to get a spreadsheet to add this column up—even sorted by customer or product group.)

The final two boxes are the key. They guide the salesperson in always defining a next step and a date that it is supposed to occur. Again, it's pretty easy to sort by date in most spreadsheet applications so you (and the salesperson) can quickly look at what is supposed to happen on all key opportunities (and when.) This not only allows you to see if progress is being made but also allows you the opportunity to intervene if you think something else needs to happen. Some organizations even link these into the calendar function so it is readily displayed for the salesperson.

The real beauty of this approach is that it only takes a few minutes a day to do call reporting because at most, you have to fill out seven boxes and after the opportunity is entered, you normally only fill out the last two.

Market information: If this is what you want, you might just want to create a question of the month program and ask everyone to ask one question per month and provide you with summarized answers. In this way, the salespeople know that it is a finite program with definite deliverables and this is probably more valuable to you anyway. (Maybe you could even have a contest and award some kind of prize to the salespeople that do the best job of gathering information.)

Temperature check: If this is what you want, why not just define the kinds of things you want to know about and let the salespeople do like the example above and give you a monthly report on the key things you want to know.

Be clear on what you want—and then establish a specific format that gets you what you want as quickly as possible with as little work as possible. You do not want to make the salespeople into market research people because this takes away from valuable sales time and gives rise to this question, "Do you want me to sell or fill out reports?"

If you ask for sales reporting, adhere to the following rules:

Start with a template. Don't let them freelance the format. Put together something that has blanks to be filled in and is easy to bring together.

Give definite due dates. If you want it every Friday, say so, and call people at home when you don't get it.

Be consistent. I can't tell you how many times some veterans are not made to comply with the rules. It's either a rule or it isn't.

Read what is submitted and provide feedback. About the only time salespeople hear from sales management about reports is when they do not do them. Take at least a minute and comment on what you read.

Use the information. If you ask the salespeople to find out the price point for a product and then ignore the information, you make them less likely to give you useful information the next time.

The bottom line on all sales reporting is that you really need to sell the value. Otherwise, it's just "busy work," and no one cares.

Section 8.7 Sales Force Automation

All of the tools mentioned previously (and others) may be considered as part of sales force automation. Like the Internet, which was supposed to replace the need for salespeople (and didn't, by the way), Sales Force Automation is supposed to have some mythical properties about it that will automatically improve sales performance and reduce the need for sales management. There are a lot of good reasons to automate some sales functions but getting a mandate from your CEO because of an article read on an airplane is not one of them.

You automate any function because of the perceived benefits. Keep in mind also that automation has two stages—doing it through technology and making it a web application. This is a formal decision that you should make, as well.

I can say one thing without equivocation about automation—your organization needs to have a website that has basic information and your people all need to have e-mail addresses. Beyond that, every additional decision to automate needs to go through the formal processes described below.

Applications

There are many parts of the sales process that can be automated:

Account information—A lot of organizations are automating their account knowledge and creating databases that allow them to slice and dice customer information. This is a valuable aid in targeting specific markets and also helps to establish things like e-mail updates lists where the right people get the right information.

Calendar/Contact Management—One of the easiest systems to put in place is an automated calendar that also drives contact management. With this in place, not only will the salespeople have a good tool to manage their time but you will also have a much clearer picture of the overall efforts of the team.

Call reporting—Many organizations allow their salespeople to enter call reports directly into their system which provides real-time call reporting and some of these systems also take key pieces out of the call report to generate other reports—thereby lessening the burden on sales time.

Marketing communications—One of the changes that may be very valuable is that some organizations are putting their brochures and catalogs on their website. And one way to ensure that presentations regarding new products and services are done correctly is to put them on a CD or on your website so that the customer gets the exact message you want to send them rather than the garbled version that might go through your sales force.

Opportunity management—Even I succumbed to the temptation and automated my opportunity management system. It started out as a hand-drawn grid, moved to a computer-drawn grid, became a simple database and is now a web application. (This application is a nice one to start with because it can be done fairly simply and in fact a lot of sales software vendors have opportunity management in their systems.)

Order entry/status/tracking—this is a no-brainer and I do not really consider it SFA at all but really part of the fulfillment piece but this is a valid application of technology, if you get something from it.

Technical data—This is another area that is only peripherally part of the sales process but if your organization has a "design in" emphasis, this might be a good thing to consider.

Automation Preparation

As stated, I am not going to make any specific recommendations because these things change so rapidly and like the Land of Oz, vendors/programs come and go so quickly here. There are a couple of recommendations that I would like to pass on:

Identify the problem before you decide on the solution. Too often the answer is "sales force automation" before we have clearly defined the question. An examples of a problem that can be solved by SFA would be that there is a need to establish a good customer database and the current system of manual entry forces salespeople out of the field for about 20% of their time. Or perhaps the opportunity management system that you are currently using is too cumbersome and you cannot get the data you need to make good market decisions. These are pretty good reasons to <u>consider </u>automation. But before you decide to automate, write down the specific problems/opportunities that will be addressed.

Do an ROI calculation. When the Great Internet Revolution was going on, one question that never was answered in a lot of companies was the Return on Investment. People were spending hundreds of thousands of dollars—or millions—out of the belief that somehow, the rules of business were now different and all you had to do was to "build it and they would come." I would recommend that you do an ROI calculation on any proposed automation effort (sales or not) and begin by determining what (if any) hard savings there are before moving on to the litany of soft value derived from the effort.

This means that if you indicate that the number of transactions per inside salesperson would be reduced by 20%, you should plan on firing 20% of the inside sales team and compute that saving—not merely assume that each person would increase their productivity by 20% and assign some magical savings number to that feat.

Do it on paper first. I would strongly recommend that you not start something in automation that you have not done using paper. It's a lot easier to automate something when the habit already exists and the use of the automated system might even be perceived as a benefit. For example, if the sales team was spending four hours a week filling out call reports and automation would save them two hours a week, this would be a good thing.

Take it in stages. Most programs of this kind look like they cost less to implement everything at once. In fact, the hard dollar costs may be better but the actual cost to your organization may be much cheaper if you implement one module at a time. (You can still buy everything and hopefully the programs are not written that require you to do everything—to do one thing.)

Manage the new habits. When you ask people to do something differently, there will always be resistance—even if there is perceived benefit. Just look at people that try to give up excessive drinking or smoking. They know it's a good idea but they don't always do it. If you want to be successful, put specific management and measurement systems in place that drive implementation. Or to put it another way, since this is a new behavior that you want, you need to do everything you can to make sure that it occurs.

Pay for the new habits. In the final section, we will discuss compensation and often, you will find that paying someone for a new behavior has value. If you incorporate the new behaviors into your compensation system, you increase the chances that the people will actually do them—with a minimum of resistance.

Measure the compliance. When you put any new program in, you should not only have measures in place but you should also analyze the results to see if they are bringing the desired benefits. There is no value in continuing to participate in a program if the benefit is not there.

One small warning: People who sell software tend to profit from the purchase of software programs. People who manage the IT departments tend to see their resources expand when your organization implements new software programs. Beware of where automation recommendations are coming from and follow the money. Who really stands to gain from the proposal? Have you already determined the answer before the question has been fully defined?

Section 8.8 Sales Measurement

In the introduction, I was at great pains to distinguish between management and measurement. The time has come to discuss the key sales measures. The point here is that you need to review some numbers in order to find problems (or opportunities). There is little purpose in gathering information unless you intend to do something with it.

The Big Picture

All sales managers need to track the Three Bs: Bookings, Billing and Backlog.

Bookings are what has been sold.
Billings are what has been billed.
Backlog is what has been sold but not billed.

A good sales manager pays attention to all three of these numbers because they provide insight into future trends.

For example, what is the appropriate ratio of bookings to billings for your business? 1:1? 1.11:1? 2:1?

These numbers reflect different sales needs. A 1:1 approach means that you are able to convert 100% of bookings into billings in the timeframe that you need and that you can maintain a relatively consistent bookings pattern. A 1.11:1 ratio means that you need an additional 10% in sales—either because you lose some percentage of booked orders or because you need to begin growing your backlog. A desired ratio of 2:1 means that you have a strong need to bill significantly better numbers and that there is a lag time between the time you book an order and the time you get to bill it.

What if you billed $1 million this month but only booked $750,000 and your billing goal is $900,000? In this case, you look great because you overachieved your billing goal by $100,000 but you depleted your backlog by $250,000 to do it. How long will you be able to book (get orders for) $750,000 and still hit your $900,000 goal? If this goes on long enough, this will create a very large hole in your billings.

The opportunity pipeline is another great set of numbers to pay attention to on a regular basis. At a minimum, you want to have an understanding of the following:

Opportunities, Qualifications and Quotes

Opportunities are the "front end" of the process where you find a piece of business to work on.

Qualifications are items such as specifications, samples and demos that generally come before an opportunity to do a real quote.

Quotes are the specific pieces of business that you have offered for sale.

In your business, there are ratios that apply. For example, what percentage of the opportunities that you find turn into qualifications? Or quotes? What percentage of qualifications turn into quotes? And finally, what percentage of quotes historically turn into sales? If you know these ratios and know what is happening in each of these areas, you can get an early warning about a whole lot of things in your business.

In the same way that you can get artificially high billings numbers by working through your backlog, you can also get artificially high booking numbers by working through your opportunity backlog. You could close most of your open quotes without replenishing them or you could convert most of your qualifications into quotes or you could convert most of your opportunities into either qualifications or quotes. All of these would give you high short term bookings numbers while creating a hole in your sales process.

There are a couple of other things that you should know here, too. How long does it take, on average, to convert an opportunity into a sale? Or a qualification into a sale? Or a quote into a sale? If you know these things, you can do a lot better job of forecasting.

If you want to get really analytical (note that anal is the root word for analytical), you can also track success by salesperson, by customer, and by product. Oh what fun you can have with that data.

At a minimum, these are the areas where you need to get some numbers.

A few additional measurements

The following are other numbers that might be good to get, if your information system lets you get them.

Strategy

The first thing that you were asked to do was to put together a matrix that was supposed to focus efforts into existing customers or new customers and existing products/services or new products/services. If you use this approach to plan, you also need to track sales in this manner—both at the company level and at the territory level. Without this on-going tracking, you will not have enough information to provide quick, accurate feedback on the sales efforts. Can you provide regular reporting using the 3x 3 matrix?

The other things that you should monitor are:

Customer mix. You had a strategy of trying to sell to specific customers. Are your opportunities coming from those customers? Or are they coming from where they have always come from?

Product mix. You wanted your sales to look a certain way. Do they? Are the opportunities that your sales team is working matching up with what you want to sell?

Margins. Margin erosion normally begins early in the process. What are the current quotes telling you about price pressures? What are the qualifications telling you? The opportunities?

Sales Planning

You were asked to establish a planning matrix for each territory that took the first matrix and made it specific by explicitly denoting what you wanted to sell and who you wanted to sell it to. As with the matrix plan, you need to be able to track the results for each box that you created. Ideally, you can track what was sold and what is in the opportunity pipeline so that you can tie results into daily activities.

Sales Process

There are some abstract numbers that are often helpful, if you can get them. This is in addition to the opportunity numbers already mentioned such as opportunities, qualifications and quotes.

The number of new account profiles entered into the system in the last 30 days is an example. If you have a prospecting goal and you use account profiles to help you manage this process, you would like to know how many new ones have been entered (and who they are.)

A second number that would be helpful is the number of account profiles that have been updated in the last 30 days (and who.) This is useful if you want to drive regular contacts with a specific group of customers and you want to know if it is occurring by monitoring the updates to the account profiles.

Another set of helpful numbers is the number of closing appointments scheduled (also who and what). If you want to check the numbers you created above concerning what is likely to book in the next 30 days, the actual scheduled closing appointments during that time are helpful. If you also know what they are trying to get orders on, this also helps you.

Sales Calls

The final area where you can use numbers to help identify problems is in the area of sales calls. In the sales management section, we referenced itineraries and call reports. If you analyze it, you might notice the average number of calls that successful salespeople make in a week. Is there a minimum? Maximum? If you look at the calls and the number is either too high or too low, you can intervene to help improve.

Another bit of analysis involves the number of planned calls that are actually made. Many salespeople put together solid weeks but then tend to accomplish only a small percentage of planned calls. If you have a salesperson that does less than 80% of what they say they will do, you have a problem there somewhere. It might be in the way the salesperson lays out their week—too little time between calls, for instance, or it might be that the salesperson always begins their days by hanging around the office so that the daily crises can be used to keep them from having to make sales calls. Either way, this kind of analysis might be helpful.

Sales Management Self-Audit

Rate each answer on a scale of 1-10 with 1 being "Not at all" and 10 being "Totally."

For each sales management tool that we use:

_____We have a specifically defined benefit.
_____The value to the salespeople has been defined.

Also,

_____We have an account information system and monitor its use and completeness.
_____We mandate the use of calendars and conduct regular reviews.
_____We have systems in place that allow us to influence sales calls before they are made.
_____We have a regular schedule of joint calls with inside/outside salespeople.
_____We have regular sales meetings, with defined agendas and timelines.
_____We are clear on what we want our sales reports to provide and give regular feedback to the salespeople on all requested information.

_____We use some form of opportunity management.
_____We have a specific set of sales measurements that help us to diagnose problems.

Add your numbers and give yourself a score: _____.

Section 9.0 Sales Training and Development

Think about your sales team and their performance. If you have more than one salesperson, you probably have a bell-shaped curve with one or two salespeople at the top who regularly produce the results you want; a larger group in the middle who sometimes are better, sometimes worse but most of the time about average; and a couple of people who are at the bottom and constantly flirt with either quitting or being fired. That's just normal, right? It's always been that way and it will always be that way. Pardon me, if I beg to differ.

Your job as sales manager is create a sales team where the lowest level of employee is average and the average is above average. This is where competitive advantage comes from—it's the one thing that no one can prevent you from doing except you. While we cannot always have the best product at the best price in large quantities, we have the option of always sending the most professional sales team to the field. (One of my guys told me once that if we would get him the best products at the best price and always have it in stock, he could sell more. I replied that if we had those things I would not need a professional sales force.)

Part of the problem with our people is one of the oldest assumptions underlying sales: Great salespeople are born and not made. Or to put it another way, selling is an art form (and therefore unmanageable.) I would actually agree with part of that thought—in that you cannot "make" a truly great salesperson because the truly great ones are, in fact, sales artists. They were born with the recognizable but un-definable quality of charisma. But that does not let you off the hook.

There is a strong process orientation in sales. I have been building on that process throughout this book. There is a process for creating a strategy—a process for sales planning—a process for organizing sales efforts—a process for selling—a process for sales calls—and a whole host of sales management processes that can be applied, given a specific set of circumstances. This is really good news when you think about it because it means that a lot of the development efforts for our salespeople can be taught (and learned.)

The teaching part is where you come in and the learning part is where the salesperson has to participate. This means that if you use a systematic approach to identifying areas of weakness and then present the salesperson with a process they can use to improve—and then monitor the process—they can improve. If it was truly just an art form, then they were either born with it or they weren't and all of your efforts would be in vain. (You're so vain, you probably think this paragraph is about you.)

There is one element that is almost (but not quite) out of your control and that is the desire of the people you are working with to be in sales. Things may have changed some over the last few years (I doubt it) but most college graduates list a career in sales just above waste treatment plant technician in terms of career choice. Remember when you came home and told your spouse you had been hired as a salesperson. Did they sigh and say something like, "Well, maybe you can get a good job soon."

This means that a lot of the raw material we have to work with may not be enthusiastic about the jobs they have. Part of this is our fault because we perpetuate the myth that you have to be born into the profession. Instead, if we show them the processes, and they see some improvement, not only will we get better salespeople but we will also make it easier for them to be more enthusiastic about choosing the "profession" of selling.

The desire to sell is the one thing that is hard for you to deal with and you should apply it in this way to your sales team:

If you have an employee who is trying (but getting less than impressive results) but they "want" to sell, you should spend a significant amount of time helping them to get there. But if both the desire and the results are lacking, perhaps you should help them to find a job for which they are better suited—riding a desk somewhere in corporate limbo-land, perhaps.

The bottom line, however, is that through your efforts, you can make poor salespeople average and average salespeople good—if they have the desire.

Section 9.1 Overview

Having waxed philosophical on the topic, you are now psychologically prepared to hear this message:

Salespeople need the same kinds of job reviews, development and training as other employees.

One of the most interesting things is that sales training was really at the forefront of the training effort in this country. Many organizations provided sales training long before they ever considered the necessity of sending executives off to leadership training.

But over the years, the application of solid human resource practices has stayed pretty constant in sales—which means that it now lags behind the efforts devoted to other areas of the organization.

Many old-line sales managers are picking themselves off the floor and muttering to themselves—why do salespeople need that kind of stuff? After all, don't they get feedback on an on-going basis from their customers—in the form of orders? Don't they get financial rewards—in the form of commission? Don't we train them well enough?

Well, maybe—and you know how I hate "maybes."

Most sales managers do some sort of sales training. A buddy call, followed by a debrief in the car at the end of the day qualifies (I have low standards for many things). Most of what passes for sales training, however, is really product training. We bring large groups of salespeople together and give them an update on the latest whizbang that we want them to push. Both of these are important but they are only part of what is required to professionally manage the sales team.

Professional management includes the following:

Formal job reviews. On an annual basis, you need to meet with each of your salespeople and review their performance and engage them in a discussion that identifies their strengths and weaknesses.

Creation of a training/development plan. After you have reviewed the entire sales team, you will have the information you need to decide how you will structure the development activities of your organization.

A formal follow-up plan. We have already discussed how joint calls and sales meetings can be part of this process. There are a few other things you need to do, as well.

If you apply formal evaluation and development processes to your salespeople (and they have a desire to be good), you can establish an on-going competitive advantage for your organization.

Section 9.2 Formal Job Rerviews

The first part of any training and development effort is to institute formal job reviews. Your company may already have a review program in place. Regardless of the process you have to go through with your company, you need to do a specific review that deals with the sales functions—and not the other stuff

Joseph C. Ellers

that they make you do—to comply with the Human Resource Department.

Knowledge, Skills, Behaviors Inventory

To do this effectively, you have to begin with the creation of the specific areas you want to evaluate. To make this easier (I hope), consider the sales job as having three different components:

Knowledge
Skills
Behaviors

Knowledge: Knowledge can be tested. This is what the salesperson needs to know to be effective. Product training is one element. Knowing how to enter an order or fill out a quote form may be others. Your first job is to list all of the specific, definable pieces of knowledge that your salespeople need to be effective.

Skills: Skills can be observed. This is the hardest part of any job to define because part of it is "artistic." Negotiating or closing are two skill-sets commonly associated with the sales profession. Think of the specific skills that your salespeople need to be effective.

Behaviors: Behaviors can be observed and counted. Normally, you can define the desired behaviors fairly easily. A sales call is a behavior. Written call plans and call reports (Boo!) are behaviors. Take a minute and list the behaviors that effective salespeople exhibit.

238

Putting these lists together are tricky because you may have some problem differentiating between the three. For example, is qualifying the customer a skill or behavior? Since I define qualifying the customer as a series of behaviors (See Step 2 of the Sales Process), I think it is a behavior but you may call it a skill. Since you're not here, I can't argue with you about it so do what you want—but be consistent.

A sample might look like this:

	Product Knowledge Widget A	Product Knowledge Widget B	Negotiating Skill	Prospecting Skill	Call Planning Behavior	Scheduled Closing Call Behavior
S Davis						
W Johnson						
A Jones						
K Smith						
L Wilson						

Once you have put this list together, you are now prepared to conduct the annual performance review.

The Review Process

Every year, you need to conduct a formal job review with each of your salespeople. Even veterans who are doing good business have some areas where they need to improve. Ideally, you would conduct these reviews around the anniversary of their hire date. This saves you from having to prepare for all of your reviews at one time.

Preparation

To do an effective performance review, you need to do the following:

Provide them with a copy of the Skills, Knowledge, Behaviors Inventory at least two weeks before you want to meet with them.

Assign them the task of rating themselves in the following manner:

++ Strong enough to teach others
+ Excellent
O Competent
-Need to improve

Also provide space for them to write general comments about their job and also specific things they would like from you over the coming year.

Mark each box yourself, using the same scoring system. If you have created your file for each salesperson, it should be pretty easy to flip back through it and look at your comments over the past year. What items did you think they did well? What areas were targeted for improvement? Did they improve? What other things did you notice that needed improvement? Which ones of those are most important to work on over the coming year?

If you conducted a formal review last year, you should also get this document out and review it—especially your comments from last year.

One of the great things about this process is that a lot of your people (even veterans) will surprise you by being tougher on themselves than you would be. Note how this will also dramatically alter the tone of the review meeting because you are not "telling" them you will be listening to them and at worst, negotiating with them over areas of improvement.

By involving them and giving them some time to prepare, you also make the review process more meaningful.

Review Meeting

There are a couple of minor points about the review meeting that you need to remember:

Schedule a specific time (and stick to it). A review meeting is the one time during the year when an employee gets a picture of their worth to the organization. If you schedule a meeting and then postpone it, you are sending the wrong message to the employee.

Do not allow yourself to be interrupted. I know it's hard to not take that phone call but when people are in a meeting that is only focused on them, you should show them how important that meeting is to you.

Do not conduct the review meeting from behind your desk. This is not the proper atmosphere if you want to get buy-in from the salesperson. Move your chair around at the very least so that you are not sitting in a potentially confrontational posture.

OK, you have done all that—now resist the urge to run down your list and tell the salesperson what you think of them. They will hear only the areas where they are negative or average and will immediately begin constructing mental defenses and tune out everything else. Instead, let them talk first. Let them go through the list and tell you what they think of themselves about each of the points. Mark their answers down next to yours and just listen. Note the areas where you agree and the areas where you disagree. And then ask them to read all of the comments they have made and take notes.

Again, you are looking for input into their thought processes as well as any comments—even constructive criticism they might have about your management style.

After listening to everything they have to say, quietly, the next step would be for you to read down the list and highlight the positive areas where you are in agreement. For example, you might list all the areas where they rated themselves a ++ or + and you agreed. (You might even have some areas where you rated them a + and they only rated themselves a 0 or competent. If this occurs, ask them why they gave themselves a lower rating than you did and see if the two of you can come to agreement on a rating.) Your goal is to build areas of agreement so that you can use this base when you move into other areas.

After you have established agreement on areas of strength, move on to agreement in areas of weakness. These would be cases where both you and the salesperson rated themselves a (-). Again, agreeing here is not seen as negative because both of you have the same rating. These are areas where you both agree that some effort needs to be placed over the coming year.

This is the easy part. The first time you do it, you might just stop there unless there are some critical areas where you think that dramatic improvement is needed and the salesperson disagrees.

Ultimately, however, you have to get to areas of disagreement. These might be areas where they think they are strong but you disagree. Or, more likely, areas where you think improvement is needed but they have rated themselves as competent.

One important point here is to have concrete examples when you disagree. As an example, one of your salespeople might say that they have excellent closing skills (+) and you might demur because they only close 12% of their quotes, as opposed to the company-wide average of 40%. In this case, you are using something that cannot be argued (too strongly) and you have removed it from simply a criticism to an observable fact.

There is nothing worse than being told that you need to improve in an area without being given specific examples. Your joint call notes will also be helpful in this regard because you should be able to quote from them as needed—and since the salesperson has been getting them along as well, there really should be no major surprises in the review meeting.

You want to use the review meeting to prioritize your efforts over the coming year. You might have selected five things where improvement is needed but you should prioritize those efforts and the two of you should agree on what the most important areas of development will be.

Post Meeting

After the meeting, you need to provide a summary to the participant. The most important action is posting the results of the review to the master development matrix because you will use this to create your training and development plan for the organization.

Section 9.3 Training and Development Plan

Once you have conducted an assessment of your people, the next step is to decide if you are going to deal with training and development issues as a group or individually. The best way to do this is to construct a Development/Training Matrix (You love a good matrix, now, don't you?) This matrix allows you to better understand the overall needs of the organization. And the real beauty is that you do not have to do any additional work—the original assessment fills in the matrix for you.

Look at the sample matrix provided below. I put together six assessment areas—these are the same used as the Knowledge, Skills and Behaviors assessment. Note that these are not necessarily detailed enough for a real evaluation but will serve for the purposes of this exercise. Then, I listed the salespeople. What does this tell you about your sales organization?

	Product Knowledge Widget A	Product Knowledge Widget B	Negotiating Skill	Prospecting Skill	Call Planning Behavior	Scheduled Closing Call Behavior
S Davis	++	+	+	0	+	-
W Johnson	+	0	++	-	0	0
A Jones	+	+	0	-	++	0
K Smith	0	-	0	0	0	-
L Wilson	-	0	0	-	0	0

As I read it, S Davis is a pretty good salesperson with only one area of real concern (Scheduled Closing Call Behavior.) Davis is also capable of providing product training on Widget A, maybe as part of a sales meeting.

W Johnson is also pretty good, with only one are of concern (Prospecting.) Johnson can be a negotiating trainer, if we need one.

A Jones is also good with only one area of need (Prospecting) and one area of training skill—Call Planning Behaviors.

K Smith and L Wilson seem to be struggling with two areas of need and competence, only, in the rest of the areas.

Each of these would need to be addressed individually, but there are also other things that this matrix tells us when we read it from top to bottom. Prospecting Skills and Scheduled Closing Call Behaviors are weak across the board and there is no internal training resource to rely on, either, so if we are going to get improvement in these areas, either the sales manager will have to provide it or maybe use outside resources such as off-the-shelf training courses or trainers.

You can see how looking at your team in this way allows you to make decisions on the best way to help them to improve their skills.

As you review the results with each salesperson you can now decide not only what to work on during the year but how you are going to attack it. For example, are you going to train the salespeople as a group—or are you going to delegate some portions of the training to individuals who have a competence in a certain area? (Don't overlook the value of getting your people involved in the training. Think of the psychological coin you get when you designate one of your people as a trainer. Not only does it make them feel good about themselves but they will also probably work extra hard in that area to justify your confidence.)

You could also decide to do one-on-one work with individuals in a few key areas.

Creation of The Plan

After you have defined the areas where you want to see improvement, you need to define the training/development activities and the follow-up system. As discussed above, there are several different ways to implement development activities:

Off-the-shelf training courses
Customized programs
Internal trainers
Sales manager
Assignments

To help you to do any of these, you need to begin with a training format. Use the one provided below as a guide:

Problem/opportunity: Define the purpose of the training.

Show them the steps: Define a process or system rather than some artform and be specific.

Give concrete examples: When you want someone to do something, give them concrete examples of when and how to use the tools you are giving them.

Describe your follow-up: Tell them how you will be looking for desired improvements.

Off-the-shelf training courses. These can be very good (or not so good) depending primarily on one thing—how clear you are on what you need. Every course is developed to solve specific problems. The key is for you to make sure that the problem they are solving is the one you have. My only problem with these types of programs is that they presume to know the answer without necessarily knowing the question. Beware of canned programs that leave blank spaces to put your examples in and are labeled custom programs. If they can show you the course materials before you buy it, it's not a custom program—although it may meet your needs.

If you are considering an off-the-shelf program, write down a list of the deliverables that you want before you start looking, then review options. If the deliverables match up what you need—go for it.

Customized programs. I have a bias on this topic because I do not really have a canned program and try to customize all of my sales training. And because of this bias, I recommend this option most of the time. The one thing to look out for, however, is that if you engage a trainer to customize the program, make sure that they have the ability to customize it. By this I do not mean that they have to have extensive knowledge in your industry—in fact this may be a detriment, but they should have a lot of related experience. (One of my beefs is that a lot of the more famous sales trainers sold consumer products rather than business-to-business products and services and there is a real difference.) Also, someone that has experience selling once in a lifetime capital products is not necessarily the person to train an industrial sales force that has to sell items everyday out of the operations budget. Your goal is to make certain that the customized program really addresses your needs (again, write down the desired deliverables before you talk with the trainer) and also that the trainer will have credibility with your team.

Internal trainers. A lot of training—especially product training—is done by internal resources. Our recommendation is that even some sales training can and should be done by those same resources. (Remember the ways it can be incorporated into sales meetings.) The only considerations here are that you should always provide very specific guidance and about what you want—and you should review the planned presentation in advance. You don't want to embarrass someone by getting them in front of the group and contradicting everything they say. (And if you assign the training to an internal resource, stay out of their way and let them do it.)

Sales manager. As the sales manager, you can do training in two different ways: as a group and on an individual basis. The matrix will give you guidance on which is most appropriate.

Assignments. For most one-on-one training or development issues, I strongly recommend assignments or SalesProjects and I have dubbed them. A sales project is just like any other project where you assign the salesperson a specific activity with the object of developing a new habit.

The format for SalesProjects looks like this:

Relate it to the performance evaluation. "I am asking you to do this because it will help you to improve your skills in the following area…"

Create a specific assignment. "Put together a list of ten target customers and present this list to me on June 1 with the reasons why you selected these ten organizations."

Provide a format. "You should present the information in this way…"

Give a due date. See above.

Follow-up when scheduled. If you asked for the assignment to be due on June 1, you need to set a specific appointment for that day to review.

Provide positive and negative feedback. No matter how poorly the person has done—especially if this is the first time—start with some part they have done well. It's easier to take a negative critique if the person knows that you are capable of providing positive reinforcements.

Section 9.4 Follow-up Plan

Your final step is to draft a formal plan that addresses all of the activities that you intend to do with a schedule of as many of the items, as possible. Part of sales management means showing the team that you have a plan and that you intend to follow it.

Sales Management Self-Audit

Rate each answer on a scale of 1-16 with 1 being "Not at all" and 16 being "Totally."

_____Our organization uses formal, annual job reviews.

_____The topics in the review are not generic, but specific to the sales function.

_____The salespeople are given a pre-meeting assignment that gets them involved in the process.

_____Our organization has a formal training and
     development plan.

_____All salespeople know exactly what they are
     expected to improve on during the coming
     year, what they need to do reach this
     improvement and how it will be monitored.

_____Sales management has a formal training and
     development calendar with activities scheduled
     throughout the year.

.

Add your numbers and give yourself a score:
_____. (Add back the 4 points I took away
from you in the scoring process. I just can't help
myself.)

Section 10.0 Sales Compensation

Almost every sales manager has some question about their sales compensation plan. Is this the best program? Should I change it? If so, what to?

Unfortunately many managers think that by simply changing the compensation plan, they can change sales behaviors. As an example, if we pay more for something, we'll get more of it, right? Maybe. Maybe not. Compensation is really just a part (an important part to be sure) but still just a part of the overall sales management process. You do need to pay for what you want, however, so that there is not an internal conflict in your sales management systems.

Some sales managers also make the flip side of this mistake by presenting new comp plans too often. (We both know that every time the comp plan is changed the salesperson thinks that the reason is to reduce their income. You wouldn't do that, would you?) To be effective, a comp plan has to be in place for multiple years. This does not mean that the objectives have to be the same but the format and rates need to be so that you can tell whether your plan is having any effect or not.

I've been involved in writing a lot of sales comp plans. When I review the existing plans, the thing that I find most often is that the plan is there because it is easy to administer. Simplicity is a good thing because if the salesperson cannot connect up what they are doing with their pay, they will not only **not** be motivated but they will in fact become de-motivated.

But think for a minute what your compensation plan is encouraging when your salespeople are paid a flat commission on all sales or all gross profit?

Many of you might be thinking: We're paying for sales, isn't that obvious? And you are, but what kind of sales? Is rebooking an existing order easier than selling a new order? Of course it is—and if I can make the same money from both, where am I likely to spend a lot of my time? Here's another question: Is it easier to sell a product or service I am familiar with or a new product or service? Again, the answer is clear and if I am paid the same for both, human nature dictates that the easiest thing for me to do is what I have always done.

Are low margin orders easier for a sales person to sell than high margin orders? Again, the answer is "yes," so once again, your system may be encouraging your salespeople to do the wrong thing. Ah, but you don't know how clever I am, you are thinking. I pay my salespeople on gross margin, not on gross sales, so that solves it, doesn't it? I mean, after all, they make more on a good margin order than a bad margin order.

Review your orders and you tell me. Do you have some dinky, non-strategic customers at the bottom of your sales list that have the same average margins as some of your better customers? Better check it out, because if you do, that part of the comp plan is not working totally well, either.

As was mentioned at the beginning, most comp plans are in place because they are easy to administer. But "easy" might not be "right." Your biggest enemy in sales management is Isaac Newton. He didn't want to be an enemy, he just put forward the theory of inertia, which means that things tend to go on like they have gone unless acted upon by an outside force—that's <u>you</u> by way: the outside force. So no matter what your compensation plan looks like, you are very likely to get more of what you have always gotten.

Section 10.1 Overview

Right about now, you're probably throwing up your hands and saying (in mild disgust), "OK, wiseguy, what sort of sales compensation plan should I have?' And the answer is one that supports your strategy and plans. Sounds simple—and it is on one level. The Devil however is in the details and there are many that have to be addressed.

Begin by defining what you want to pay for…

The first step in creating the "right" compensation plan for your organization is to review what you want more (and less) of.

Start by reviewing the company-wide sales matrix. What do you want that is different from what you have?

Sales of new products or services?
To new customers?
At better margins?

If you look at your answers, you can see what you really want: sales of specific products or services to specific customers at specific margins. Now, the key

Joseph C. Ellers

question, how much of the sales force compensation should come from selling those things?

A lot of sales compensation plans really reward retention more than anything else. In other words, most of their compensation will come from salary and commissions/bonus on rebooking orders we already have at customers we also already have (at margins we already have—or less). If this is the most important strategic activity to your organization, then this is the right answer, by the way. But what if it isn't? What if your salespeople really do need to be focused on selling differently?

How would you structure the compensation plan to make more of their pay dependent on getting the right results? What if, for instance, you paid a significant bonus commission on new sales to new customers at the right margins and regular commission on everything else? In this way, you would at least be reinforcing the message that you are trying to send (without hurting the salespeople in any way.)

We can also take it one step further—will different activities be required to get different results? If so, you might consider paying something for the right activities—not just the right results but more about that later.

The bottom line on sales compensation plans is that effective plans have the following components:

The organization is very clear on what it wants and pays more for what it wants more of. **So if the** organization wants new customers, the pay is higher for new customers than existing customers.

The plan drives the <u>activities</u> required to accomplish the results. If the organization wants sales from new customers, the salesperson understands that additional/better quality prospecting activities are required.

The salesperson can clearly connect what they do with what they get. The commission report clearly connects what the organization says it wants with the pay the salesperson receives. If the salesperson has to get you to interpret the commission statement, you have not done this part right.

The salesperson trusts your reports. If the salesperson does not trust the commission reports, they will expend a lot of energy checking your numbers and there will be no real drive from the plan.

The compensation comes often enough so that there is a direct correlation between their results and the pay. For most people, an annual bonus is just too far away to have much impact on daily behaviors. This is especially true of less seasoned salespeople.

The plan is part of an overall sales management plan designed to push/pull everyone in the same direction. Of all the points in this discussion, this one may be the most important. You cannot rely on the compensation plan alone to get the sales results you want. Even great comp plans sometimes fail to get the desired results because the organization (or sometimes even the sales manager) sends out contradictory messages.

For example, if you have focused the salesperson on new customer sales but every time the salesperson has a day of prospecting work scheduled, you redirect them into calls on existing customers, you are undoing the effects of the compensation plan. The organization sometimes fights against the efforts as well, for instance, when orders from new customers are always put on backorder to support the existing customer base.

Your goal as a sales manager is to use everything we have discussed so far to put together a plan that hangs together—with compensation as a final kicker. For as the great American patriot Ben Franklin once said, "If we don't hang together, we shall all hang separately."

Section 10.2 Salary versus Commission vs Bonus

There are three ways that you can pay salespeople—salary, commission and bonus.

Each of these elements sends a different message about what you want the salesperson to do. (You also get different types of salespeople based on your comp plan and further, you get different results from different kinds of people—based on the structure of your plan). Begin the thought process by thinking about those three items as comprising a pie chart— what percentage of sales comp do you want to pay for each of these three components?

Salary: The regular pay that people get every month whether they sell anything or not.

Commission: Variable amount paid for sales results.

Bonus: A specific amount of money paid for some specifically defined result (hopefully).

Look a the different messages you send, just by changing the weighting of the various components:

Salary 90%
Commission 0%
Bonus 10%

Salary 0%
Commission 90%
Bonus 10%

Salary 50%
Commission 45%
Bonus 5%

Each of these is an appropriate compensation strategy, given some different sets of circumstances.

Salary: A high salary has two primary uses—to support pioneering activities and to encourage high service levels in existing accounts. (Some managers also use salaries to encourage team behaviors since salespeople are less vehement about protecting their client base if they are not paid directly on the results.)

Pioneering activities means opening new territories. If you have a territory with little or no existing revenue, it's not really fair to pay someone on commission (unless they can make very quick sales that pay a lot of commission.) You cover that by agreeing to pay a salary for some pre-determined and agreed upon time period—if you expect them to convert to commission/bonus at some point.

The second main reason to use high salaries involves the need for high service levels on existing business. The baseline might be the need to work on retention or it could be that the sales job is really more a field customer service or technical support job as described in Section 3.0.

If your needs are other than these, you might want to consider making the other components higher.

Commission

Commission is the most common form of sales compensation. Comp plans that have a high commission component are generally used to drive sales—all sales—rather than specific sales, unless the commission plan is modified, based on results. (For instance a bonus commission of 10% on sales to new customers, as mentioned previously.)

One problem with some commission-driven plans, however, is that they often cease to drive behaviors. As an example, if your product is a product that is used by the customers on a regular basis (like a lot of industrial distribution products), you may have a plan where the salesperson gets 100% of their pay through commission. In this case, you would think that the salesperson is motivated to do selling behaviors, but in fact, they know that a large part of their income is quasi-guaranteed because they will get a lot of reorders during the year from existing customers. In this case, they will have a tendency to be more focused on making sure they visit existing customers and talk about what they already sell than make any kind of effort to sell new things.

Another commission consideration involves how often you pay it. If you are dealing with a junior salesperson, you might pay commission on a weekly basis to provide frequent positive reinforcement of good behaviors. Commission plans that are paid quarterly can only be used with mature salespeople who can take a longer view. Annual commission plans are not really commission plans at all but more like bonuses because the connection between what the salespeople do and their reward is too far apart for the commission to be motivational or directional.

Bonus

Compensation plans that have a high bonus content are normally used to reward longer term objectives— sometimes activity-driven rather than results-driven. Bonuses are generally paid on a quarterly basis and some are annual. Understand that a bonus commission is not a bonus. So for example, if you were going to pay a salesperson 10% for sales and you pay an additional 1% for sales of a certain product, that is not a bonus but bonus commission—and therefore commission.

Examples of bonuses would be:

$10,000 if a certain threshold of sales is hit
$5,000 if the salesperson does at least ten new product demos, per quarter
$1,000 if sales of a certain product hit a minimum
$1,000 if 10 new customers place orders during a quarter

Note that there is a minimum but the bonus amount does not go up if the salesperson overachieves the targets. (If the bonus does go up, then it is a form of commission.)

Bonuses are generally used to direct a salesperson to achieve a minimum of something in a defined time period.

As a sales manager, your first question is to determine which kind of compensation plan supports your organization's strategy and goals. The second issue is to understand the people you have and the people you need to execute these goals.

One way of describing the different types of salespeople is in terms of hunters and farmers. Hunters have strengths in finding new customers and new opportunities and in fact they thrive in that environment. Farmers do better in working a particular patch of ground. They can grow sales, too, but their growth will mainly come from the plot they are working and it might come a bit slower, too.

Remember, that as you are putting together your comp plan that no plan will convert one kind of person into the other. You might be able to get a little more farming out of a hunter and little more hunting out of a farmer, but at the end of the day, you will still have the hunters and farmers you started out with.

The final consideration in this section is to make certain that your people and your strategies line up and not to expect to change a person's behaviors too dramatically—no matter how you pay them.

Section 10.3 Results versus Activities

Most sales comp plans are based on results. This makes sense, especially if the salespeople are already doing the activities needed to produce the results you want.

When you want different things, however, you might want to consider paying for changed behaviors in addition to changed results.

At base, this is what a manager really does, anyway. Managers are supposed to influence activities. The manufacturing manager does not manage the finished goods, they manage the people and processes designed to make the finished goods. In some ways, sales managers often fall into the trap of trying to manage the finished goods (sales) rather than the people/processes that produce them.

This is part of the distinction that has been discussed previously where I climbed on my soapbox to discuss the difference between management (directing activities) and measurement (looking backward at results.)

Consider just the three kinds of things we talked about previously that you might want to be different:

New customer sales
New product/service sales
Higher margins

Your plan can either pay for results or the activities that produce them. (Or some of each. But that will be covered in the last section.)

Compensating for Results

Using the three desired results presented above, the following can be used:

New customer sales: One of the simplest ways to compensate for results is to pay either higher commission or bonuses based on sales that come from new customers. As an example, if you pay 5% on sales to existing customers and 15% on sales to new customers, you are certainly sending a message about your focus on new customers.

Some organizations also do this through bonuses. One example would be to pay a bonus of $100.00 for every order that comes from a new customer or to pay a bonus of $1000 for every $10,000 of sales from new customers.

The ultimate way to focus salespeople on new customers is to pay them nothing on existing business (the salary they receive is compensation for service activities) with all commission coming from sales to new customers. This is not a recommendation—just a look at the different messages that you can send by compensating for results.

New product/service sales: As with the example above, you can easily pay higher commissions on sales of new products or services. Or bonuses, based on sales of new products or even based on hitting certain targets. For example, you might pay a $1000 bonus if the salesperson hits a target of $50,000 in new product sales.

Higher margins: One of the fallacies of compensation is that if you pay 10% of gross margin in commission that you are paying for higher margins. After all, 10% of $250 is bigger than 10% of $200. But when you analyze it, the real kicker would look more like this—pay 5% of gross margin if the gross margin percentage is up to 20% and pay 10%, if it's over 20%. This really pays the salesperson to get better margins because their compensation more than doubles.

If you are concerned about margins, you cannot have any pay plan that does not address margin percentage. In other words, a plan that pays on gross sales or gross margin without factoring in margin percentage will encourage higher sales at lower margins.

Some organizations also address this point by paying higher commission in products that naturally carry higher margins. This is especially true if the salespeople have little control over margin percentage but the organization still needs to increase margins. For example, we sell five items and one of them has an average gross margin of 30% and the rest have gross margins of 20%. You could pay 10% on the 20% items and 20% on the 30% item. In this way, you are driving the salespeople toward what you say you want more of.

Compensating for Activities

In addition to (or instead of) compensating for the results, you can also pay for the activities that are likely to produce the results you want.

New customer sales: There are several activities that drive this result—all of them under the general heading of prospecting. Salespeople can be tasked to put together prospect customer lists, do research, make survey calls, and fill out account profiles. These are all quantifiable activities that the sales manager can direct rather than a result.

As an example, you could pay a salesperson a bonus commission of 1% on all sales if they do a minimum of 5 survey calls on new customers per week. Or you could pay a bonus of $1000 if they complete 20 account profiles on new customers during the first quarter.

New product/service sales: There are multiple activities that can help get these results. Salespeople can be tasked to take specific product training classes, identify new people (with different job titles) within their customer base, make initial calls on these new people, make specific presentations and present specifications and samples of new/different products. Again, these are quantifiable activities, that if done properly, should aid in getting the different results desired by the sales manager.

One approach would be to pay a bonus commission of 1% on sales of certain products if the salesperson attends a certain number of training classes for the product. Or you could pay a bonus of $1000 if the salesperson identifies 50 design engineers within ten target companies that make the decision on whether your product is specified.

Higher margins: Higher margins come from calling on different customers and presenting different products than are currently being presented. But higher margins also come from calling on different people and making different kinds of presentations. Remember our chart in Section 6 where we talked about the salesperson's ability to influence the sale and the relative importance of price and availability? You may also be able to get better margins by teaching your people negotiation skills or by better educating them on the real competitive issues in the customer base. Again, all of these are activities and not results.

And you could pay a bonus commission if the salesperson makes 25 product presentations within the quarter or a bonus of $1000 if the salesperson takes the negotiating course that you have been recommending.

The good news is that you can direct the activities of your salespeople by paying for results and activities. The bad news is that it often rankles people to pay for activities.

Section 10. 4 Sales MBO Plans

One of the problems of sales compensation plans is that the plans are easy to administer because they are the same for everyone. But how often do your salespeople really have the exact same situation?

An MBO plan provides the manager with the ability to customize the comp plan for every individual—without really having different plans. This approach also allows you to change the emphasis every year without changing the plan. You can implement an MBO plan now—no matter what current plan you use—because the format presented is really additional compensation that focuses on what you want more of—so you are taking nothing away—simply adding to what they already get. This approach cuts down on complaints.

In the example presented below, the sales manager has two salespeople and wants to provide the same basic compensation plan—with some issues that are the same—and some that are different. Note also that the MBO plan is a mix of commission and bonus—and a mix of compensation to drive results and activities.

Salesperson 1:

In this instance, the manager wants to address lack of sales of certain products; lack of retention efforts in existing accounts; and regular use of survey calls.

Basic commission plan pays 5% of gross margin on a monthly basis

Bonus commission of 1% for sales of product A, B and C (because this salesperson is not selling the appropriate percentage of each of these products.)

Bonus commission of 1% on sales of focus customers (because this salesperson is losing sales in their key accounts.)

Bonus of $500 per quarter if the salesperson completes a minimum of 4 survey calls, per month.

Bonus of $1000 if sales of products A, B and C hit their minimum established targets.

Salesperson 2:

In this instance, the manager wants to address lack of sales in specific areas (slightly different than Salesperson 1) and prospecting activities.

Basic commission plan pays 5% of gross margin on a monthly basis

Bonus commission of 1% for sales of product C, D and E (because this salesperson is not selling the appropriate percentage of each of these products.)

Bonus commission of 1% on sales of new customers (because this salesperson is not spending enough effort in finding new customers.)

Bonus of $500 per quarter if the salesperson completes a minimum of 4 survey calls, per month.

Bonus of $1000 if sales of products C, D and E hit their minimum established targets.

You can see that this is the same plan but it rewards different things. If you are considering moving to some sort of MBO program, you need to think about the following:

You have to be very clear on exactly what you need from each territory.

You have to have systems in place to measure what you want.

You have to pay attention to these things, on a regular basis. Remember that simply putting this program in place will not get you the results you want. You have to couple any compensation plan with a management plan that is also pointing in the same direction.

Sales Management Self-Audit

Rate each answer on a scale of 1-16 with 1 being "Not at all" and 16 being "Totally."

_____The organization is very clear on what it wants and pays more for what it wants more of.

_____The plan drives the activities required to accomplish the results.

_____The salespeople can clearly connect what they do with what they get.

_____The salespeople trust their commission reports.

_____The compensation comes often enough so that there is a direct correlation between their results and the pay.

_____The plan is part of an overall sales management plan designed to push/pull everyone in the same direction.

Add your numbers and give yourself a score: _____. (OK, one last time, give yourself 4 points.)

Appendices

To Achieve Better Results Quicker, Send For Free Supplements

We've made it so easy for you to succeed that it's virtually impossible not to get better results if you follow the steps detailed in this book accurately.

And to make it even more valuable, we've added some supplemental materials to make implementing these concepts easy and hassle free.

Sales Forms- Emailed to you FREE

Send us an email and we'll send you our *Forms-On-CD.* The same forms you see in the appendix Totally FREE so you can customize & duplicate them for easy use.

Receive these forms Free, email us at: joeellers@aol.com

Additional *Sales Management Handbook* Materials...

The Sales Manager's Workbook

If you really want to get this concepts down-cold, try using our Workbook. It will take you through various situations and scenarios enabling you to really work through some of these concepts on paper, before using them in the field. This will help you become ultra-prepared to start getting the results that are truly possible.

For additional information email us at: joeelers@aol.com

Book-on-Tape / CD

The information in this book is so powerful, that you'll want to review it over and over so you drill it into your brain for permanent use. **Our New Book-on-Tape.** Now you can listen at home or in your car.

For additional information email us at: joeelers@aol.com

Feel Free to Contact Us Any Time
About This Publication or Other Books
& Products by Joseph Ellers.
joeelers@aol.com

Appendix 1. My Sales Management Action Plan

Based on the changed results we want, we will make the following changes:

Do some things you have never done before

Do some things you are already doing more often

Do some things you are already doing differently

Stop (or significantly curtail) doing some things you are currently doing

Appendix 2. Strategic Planning Questionnaire

Give these questions as many people as are appropriate in your organization. Compile the results and use them to help drive the accompanying agenda.

Question 1. What will we look like in 3-5 years? Write a 2-3 sentence paragraph that describes how the business will look.

Question 2: How much do we want to grow? How profitable do we want to be?

Think of this question as a pie chart. What percentage of our total company efforts should be devoted to growing the top line and what percentage should be devoted to the bottom line? Example—top line 54%, bottom line 46%.

Question 3: What is our core strategy?

To be successful, a business generally has to pick one area of focus. There are three basic areas:

1) Efficiency
2) Innovation
3) Intimacy

Which one of these areas will be most important to the future success of the organization?

Question 4: How do we want to grow?

Put a dollar amount in each of these boxes that indicates how much business you intend to get from each of these sources next year. Three years from now.

Raise prices	Existing products/services	New products/services
Existing customers		
New Customers		

Question 5: What do we want to sell?

Question 6: Who do we want to sell it to?

Question 7: What does a good order look like?

Question 8: What is really important?

Rank the following in order of importance:

_____Short-term billings

_____Quality
_____Customer service
_____Controlling costs
_____Increased productivity
_____Long-term profits
_____Innovation

Question 9: What do we reward people for?

Question 10: SWOT Analysis?

List the most important item in each of these categories:

Strengths

Weaknesses:

Opportunities:

Threats:

Question 11: What do we need to invest in?

Appendix 3. Strategic Planning Agenda

Introductory Remarks

Section 1. Brief Review of Survey Results

Based on your review of the survey summary, what, if any, topics need to be discussed at this meeting?

Section 2. Creation of Long-term Vision

How big do we want to be?

How profitable?

New markets/products?

New technologies/products?

Structural changes?

Other?

Joseph C. Ellers

Section 3. Definition of Short/Long-term Sales Targets

Next year:

Raise Prices	Existing Products	New Products
Existing Customers		
New Customers		

What activities are required to support these goals?

Three years:

Raise Prices	Existing Products	New Products
Existing Customers		
New Customers		

What activities are required to support these goals?

Section 4. Definition of Key Strategic Business Initiatives

Based on our discussions so far, what are the 3-5 areas of focus for the next 12-18 months?

Sample Activities Assignment:

Initiative	Activity	Responsible	Due	Status
Introduce New Whizbang	Identify target market	Jim S	7-01	
	Develop engineering budget	Mary D	7-31	
	Product prototype	Paul J	10-31	
	Tradeshow introduction	Susan Q	12-10	

Section 5. Roll-out Plan

What is the target complete date?

What do we intend to share?

What format will we use to share?

Joseph C. Ellers

<u>Appendix 4. Strategic Sales Growth Matrix</u>

	Existing Products	New Products
Existing Customers		
New Customers		

Appendix 5. Sales Organization Design Tools

Figure 1: Where are you? Where do you need to be?

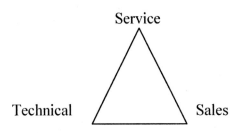

Figure 2: Where are you?   Where do you need to be?

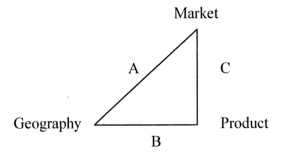

Joseph C. Ellers

Figure 3. Channel Mix Matrix

	Percent through channel
Direct	
Reps	
Distribution	

Figure 4. Where are you? Where do you want to be?

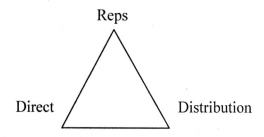

Figures 5-9. Where are you? Where do you need to be?

Inside--Outside

Counter sales—customer service—telesales—inside sales

Formal pairs-------------------------------Random access

Inside
Few assigned accounts---------Many assigned accounts

Outside
Few assigned accounts---------Many assigned accounts

Appendix 6. Sales Personnel Assessment Tools

Figure 1. Where are you? Where do you nd to be?

Reactive--Proactive

Figure 2. Sales Personnel Needs Matrix

Category	Outside	Inside
Sales		
Technical		
Service		
Geography		
Market		
Product		
Route driver		
Lit fairy		
Visitor		
Outside CS		
Sales		
Counter		
Service		
Telesales		
Inside sales		
Proactive Rating		
Formal Partnering		
Random		
Mostly salary		
Mostly commission		

Figure 3. The Selection Process Checklist

Applicant: _____

_____Review the resume and look for a lot of job changes.

_____Look for the type of work experience you want

_____Ask to review their calendars.

_____Look for people who have a desire to sell.

_____Ask them what they will be earning in three to five years.

_____Ask them how they feel about quotas/goals.

_____Listen for references to "team" selling.

_____Ask them about life goals

_____Ask them to sell you something.

_____Ask them the reason they are leaving their current job.

Total score:_____

Joseph C. Ellers

Appendix 7. Sales Strategic Planning Matrix

	Product A	Product B	Service C	Product D
Customer 1				
Customer 2				
Prospect 3				
Customer 4				

Appendix 8. Summary of Sales Process Questions

Step One Summary Questions

How much time does each salesperson need to spend on finding new customers?

Which prospects seem to meet our definition of "good?" Are there enough of them?

What is our process for learning about customers? What do we need to know about them, upfront?

Are the salespeople doing the things they need to do?

Are they getting the right results or do you need to work with some of them to help them improve their prospecting skills?

Step Two Summary Questions

What process do they use to buy what you are selling?

Who is involved?

How does the requisition/specification process work?

What half of the equation (TAC vs PUC) has the power in this transaction?

Step Three Summary Questions

What kind of opportunities are your salespeople supposed to find?

What activities is your salesperson supposed to do to find opportunities?

Are they doing them? Enough of them? Well enough?

What activities is your salesperson supposed to do to determine the "reality" of each opportunity?

Are they doing them? Enough of them? Well enough?

Step Four Summary Questions

Does what we are proposing address the customer's concerns?

Does the salesperson understand how the customer will answer this question?

What are the activities that your salespeople must do to help the customer decide if our product/service meets their needs?

What are the customer activities that are required to determine if your product or service meets their needs? Who is involved in these processes?

How do they evaluate:

Our product/service?
Our company?
The salesperson?

What is the pattern of objections? In the territory? At specific customers?

Step Five Summary Questions

Is the opportunity really at the quote/proposal stage?
  Is this a quote for buy, budget, ballpark or blowoff?

What kind of activities are required?
Does this opportunity warrant a quote or proposal?
What should be in the proposal?

Are the quotes reflective of our strategy?
Are your salespeople quoting the right kinds of orders? Are they beginning to look more like what you want?

Step Six Summary Questions

Are the closing attempts occurring at the right time?

Are the closing attempts done correctly?
  Is the close scheduled?
  Is a closing question asked?

Are you managing the process? Pay attention to the following:
  Scheduled closing calls
  Effectiveness, by category
  Margins

Appendix 9. Perfect Sales Call Summary Questions

Sales Call Problem Analysis Summary Questions

What is their current approach for trying to get sales appointments?

Are their signs that there is a problem:

> No "need" for scheduled calls?

> Inability to schedule calls?

> Customer-blown appointments?

> Lobby calls?

> Long waits?

Preparation Summary Questions

What does the salesperson want to accomplish?

Can the salesperson present the customer's value?

Do they review their account knowledge before trying to schedule the call?

Are they scheduling "real" sales calls?

Do they use written call plans?

Do they have what they will need to complete the call objectives?

Sales Call Summary Questions

Does the salesperson have "real" sales calls? Are they on the right customers?

Are they spending sales time making calls or doing service activities?

How are they doing on the "quality" issues:

>   Punctuality?

>   Following the plan?

>   Accomplishing objectives?

Defining the next step?

Are they calling on enough of the right people on the call?

How do they do on the "mechanics?"

Do they need to work on the personal attributes?

Follow-up Summary Questions

What does the salesperson do immediately after the call?

Are they putting off until tomorrow something that would be done much better today?

Appendix 10. Joint Call Checklist

Salesperson: _____

Date: _____

Calls: _____

1) Number of calls with a sales purpose planned (5 points maximum)

    Sales purpose means trying to sell something—not a customer service call) Grade:

    _____

2) 1st/last call schedule (5 points maximum)

    (Before 8:30/after 4:00—5 points) (Before 9:30/after 3:00—0 points)
    Grade: _____

3) Call plans (10 points maximum)

    (Written call plans for all calls—5 points)) (No calls—0 points)
    Grade: _____

4) Call schedule quality (10 points maximum)

   (Date/time/purpose—all   calls—10   points)
   (Never—0 points)
   Grade: _____

5) Personal (3 points maximum per category)

   Appearance _____
   Calendar _____
   Note-taking ability _____
   Literature/samples _____

6) Profiles (3 points maximum per category)

   Exist_____
   Substantially complete for major customers
   _____
   Use to prepare for call_____
   Updated (as appropriate) after each call
   _____

7) Account Penetration (4 points maximum per category)

   Multiple contacts _____
   Strategic contacts _____

8) Sales Calls (3 points maximum per category)

Punctual _____
Followed call plan _____
Accomplished objectives _____
Scheduled Next Step _____

9) Mechanics (3 points maximum per category)
Opening _____
Presentation _____
Questioning _____
Listening _____
Overcoming objections _____
Closing _____

10) Other (8 points maximum)

Total Points: _____

General comments:

Activities for future follow-up:

Next scheduled review date:

<u>Appendix 11. Opportunity Management Report</u>

Date in	Customer	Contact	Opportunity	Value	Next step	Date

For more information on this tool, go to oppmanager.com

<u>Appendix 12. Training and Development Tools</u>

Figure 1. Knowledge, Behavior and Skills Inventory Matrix

Salesperson	Product Knowledge Widget A	Product Knowledge Widget B	Negotiating Skill	Prospecting Skill	Call Planning Behavior	Scheduled Closing Call Behavior

Figure 2. Development Format Questions

Problem/opportunity: Define the purpose of the training.

Show them the steps: Define a process or system rather than some artform and be specific.

Give concrete examples: When you want someone to do something, give them concrete examples of when and how to use the tools you are giving them.

Describe your follow-up: Tell them how you will be looking for desired improvements.

Figure 3. SalesProjects Format

Relate it to the performance evaluation. "I am asking you to do this because it will help you to improve your skills in the following area..."

Create a specific assignment. "Put together a list of ten target customers and present this list to me on June 1 with the reasons why you selected these ten organizations."

Provide a format. "You should present the information in this way..."

Give a due date. See above.

Follow-up when scheduled. If you asked for the assignment to be due on June 1, you need to set a specific appointment for that day to review.

Joseph C. Ellers

About the Author

Joseph C. Ellers was born in Morgantown, West Virginia in 1959. He attended Clemson University, graduated from Southern Wesleyan University and was awarded a Doctorate of Human Letters from the Kutaisi State Technical University.

Since founding Palmetto Associates in 1987, Ellers has worked with hundreds of businesses – in almost every industry, throughout the world.

Most clients have been in the business-to-business arena and have come from the following industries: aerospace, apparel, architecture, automotive, carpet, distribution, electronics, engineering, food, furniture, gas, industrial equipment, medical, metal-working, motor repair, packaging, pharmaceuticals, power transmission, publishing, software, steel, telecommunications, textiles, tobacco, tradeshows, and utilities.

In addition, Ellers has worked with numerous distribution associations to provide specialized consulting and training to their memberships. These associations include the American Supply Association, Electrical Apparatus Service Association, Electronic Distribution Management Association, Electronic Representatives Association, Industrial Distribution Association, International Sanitary Supply Association, National Electronics Distribution Association and the Steel Service Center Institute.

He also has associations with the Industrial Distribution Program at the University of Alabama-

Birmingham and the Industrial Extension Department at North Carolina State University.

In 1996, Ellers was elected to the Russian Academy of Quality Problems

His other books include:

Getting to Know Clemson University...(1987)

Market-Driven Manufacturing (with F. Paul Clipp) 1990

Strom Thurmond: The Public Man (1993)

American Government: The Case for a Return to Federalism (2000)

In addition, he has other publications including:

Coauthorship of numerous courses for the National Management Association including *Implementing Process Improvement* (1994).

Numerous articles for various publications including: "Better Repping," Bobbin, *Electronic Distribution Today*, *The Networker*, *Prescriptions & Descriptions*, *The PT Distributor*, *Quality Digest, Southern Purchaser, Textile Manufacturing*, and *Tradeshow Week*.

Winner of Gold and Silver Awards in the 22nd Annual Editorial Excellence Competition (ASBPE) for articles written in 1999 for Tradeshow Week.

Songwriting: "Special Light of Christmas," *God Gives Songs for Kids (4),* Uniting Church of Australia, 1998.

Video: *The Perfect Sales Call* with Joe Ellers; 2000, Produced by Success Video Productions.

Ellers makes his home in Clemson, SC.